ROSA PARKS:

MY STORY

Throughout her arrest for participating in the Montgomery Bus Boycott, Rosa Parks maintained her dignity. (Courtesy of The Schomburg Center, NYPL)

ROSA PARKS:

MY STORY

by Rosa Parks

with Jim Haskins

Dial Books
New York

Published by Dial Books
A Division of Penguin Books USA Inc.
375 Hudson Street
New York, New York 10014

Library of Congress Cataloging in Publication Data
Parks, Rosa, 1913–
Rosa Parks: my story/with Jim Haskins.
p. cm.
ISBN 0-8037-0673-1
1. Parks, Rosa, 1913–   2. African-Americans—Alabama—
Montgomery—Biography.
3. Civil rights workers—Alabama—Montgomery—Biography.
4. Segregation in transportation—Alabama—Montgomery—
History—20th century.
5. African-Americans—Civil rights—Alabama—Montgomery—
History—20th century.
6. Montgomery (Ala.)—Biography. I. Haskins, James, 1941–   II. Title.
F334.M753P37 1992 976.1'47—dc19 [B] 89-1124 CIP

This book is dedicated to the memory of
my mother, Leona McCauley,
and my husband, Raymond A. Parks.

I am grateful to Elaine Steele, my friend,
traveling companion, and Executive Director of
the Rosa and Raymond Parks Institute for
Self-Development, for her help with this book.

To Rosa Parks
Whose creative witness was the great force that led to the
modern stride toward freedom

Martin L. King, Jr.

—Inscription written by Dr. King on the frontispiece
of his book Stride Toward Freedom, *a copy of which*
he gave to Rosa Parks.

CONTENTS

1

How It All Started

One evening in early December 1955 I was sitting in the front seat of the colored section of a bus in Montgomery, Alabama. The white people were sitting in the white section. More white people got on, and they filled up all the seats in the white section. When that happened, we black people were supposed to give up our seats to the whites. But I didn't move. The white driver said, "Let me have those front seats." I didn't get up. I was tired of giving in to white people.

"I'm going to have you arrested," the driver said.

"You may do that," I answered.

Two white policemen came. I asked one of them, "Why do you all push us around?"

He answered, "I don't know, but the law is the law and you're under arrest."

For half of my life there were laws and customs in the South that kept African Americans segregated from Caucasians and allowed white people to treat black people without any respect. I never thought this was fair, and from the time I was a child, I tried to protest against disrespectful treatment. But it was very hard to do anything about segregation and racism when white people had the power of the law behind them.

Somehow we had to change the laws. And we had to get enough white people on our side to be able to succeed. I had no idea when I refused to give up my seat on that Montgomery bus that my small action would help put an end to the segregation laws in the South. I only knew that I was tired of being pushed around. I was a regular person, just as good as anybody else. There had been a few times in my life when I had been treated by white people like a regular person, so I knew what that felt like. It was time that other white people started treating me that way.

One of my earliest memories of childhood is hearing my family talk about the remarkable time that a white man treated me like a regular little girl, not a little black girl. It was right after World War I, around 1919. I was five or six years old. Moses Hudson, the owner of the plantation next to our land in Pine Level, Alabama, came out from the city of

Montgomery to visit and stopped by the house. Moses Hudson had his son-in-law with him, a soldier from the North. They stopped in to visit my family. We southerners called all northerners Yankees in those days. The Yankee soldier patted me on the head and said I was such a cute little girl. Later that evening my family talked about how the Yankee soldier had treated me like I was just another little girl, not a little black girl. In those days in the South white people didn't treat little black

Rosa Parks's birthplace in Tuskegee, Alabama. (Courtesy of Rosa Parks)

children the same way as little white children. And old Mose Hudson was very uncomfortable about the way the Yankee soldier treated me. Grandfather said he saw old Mose Hudson's face turn red as a coal of fire. Grandfather laughed and laughed.

I was raised in my grandparents' house in Pine Level, in Montgomery County, near Montgomery, Alabama. All my mother's people came from Pine Level. My mother's name was Leona Edwards. My father

Rosa's mother, Leona Edwards (seated); and Leona's cousin Beatrice. (Courtesy of Rosa Parks)

Rosa's father, James McCauley, 1923. (Courtesy of Rosa Parks)

came from Abbeville, Alabama. His name was James McCaulcy. He was a carpenter and a builder, very skilled at brick- and stonemasonry. He traveled all around building houses.

My father's brother-in-law, Reverend Dominick, Aunt Addie's husband, was pastor of the Mount Zion African Methodist Episcopal Church in Pine Level, and it was there in Pine Level that my father met my mother, who was a teacher. They were married right there in Pine Level on April 12, 1912. My mother was twenty-four years old, and my father was the same age.

After they were married, they moved to Tuskegee, Alabama, to live. It was the home of Tuskegee Institute, which Mr. Booker T. Washington had founded back in 1881 as a school for blacks. My parents lived not far from it. Both black and white leaders called the town of Tuskegee a model of good race relations, and that may have been why my father wanted to move there. And there were a lot of building jobs in the county of Macon, Alabama. My mother got a job teaching.

It wasn't long before they started a family. I was born on February 4, 1913, in Tuskegee, and named Rosa after my maternal grandmother, Rose. My mother was around twenty-five years old by the time I was born, but she always said that she was unprepared to be a mother. I guess she was unhappy because my father worked on building homes in different places in the county and she was left alone quite a bit. She had to quit teaching until after I was born, and she always talked about how unhappy she was, being an expectant mother and not knowing many people. At that time women who were pregnant didn't get out and move around and socialize like they do now. They stayed pretty much to themselves. She said she spent a lot of time crying and weeping and wondering what she was going to do and how she was going to get along, because she wasn't used to having a child to take care of.

I came along and I was a sickly child, small for

Robert McCauley, Rosa's uncle, sent this postcard of a house he was building to her father, James McCauley, asking about the family. (Courtesy of Rosa Parks)

my age. It was probably hard for my mother to take care of me. And my father's younger brother came to live with us, so that was someone else to cook and wash for. My uncle Robert was a carpenter too, and he enrolled at Tuskegee Institute to take courses in carpentry and building. But my mother always said Uncle Robert knew so much about what they were trying to teach him that he was teaching the instructors. Every time they would say something about a building plan, he would say, "No, I think we should arrange to do it this way," and then they would arrange it the way he suggested and it would come out right. He didn't stay at Tuskegee Institute very long as a student.

I have pictures of the houses my father and my uncle built—beautiful houses. They learned from their father, I think. They didn't learn anything at Tuskegee.

But Tuskegee was still the best place in Alabama for African Americans to get an education, and my mother wanted to stay there. Her idea was for my father to take a job at Tuskegee Institute. Teachers got houses to live in at that time, so they would have a place to stay. The other children they would have and I would get an opportunity for an education at the Institute. At that time black children in the South had very limited opportunities for schooling. But my father didn't go along with that idea. He wanted to do contracting work and make more money. He and my mother didn't agree on planning for the future.

My father decided he didn't want to remain in Tuskegee. He wanted to go back to his family in Abbeville. My mother had no choice but to go with him.

So we went to Abbeville to live with my father's family. It was a big family, with lots of children. My grandmother had started having children early and didn't stop for a long time. When I was born, my father's youngest brother, George Gaines Mc-Cauley, was eight years old. He used to tell me he was jealous of me because he'd been the baby for eight years and he didn't like me as a new baby at all. But he liked me as I grew older.

I learned all I know about my father's family from my young uncle George. He said that my father's grandfather was unknown and someone said he was one of the Yankee soldiers who served in the South during the Civil War. My father's grandmother was a slave girl and part Indian or something. That's all I know. If my mother knew more than that, she never told me. I guess she felt she wasn't as compatible with that family as she should have been with her in-laws.

I think my mother may have done some teaching in Abbeville, but she didn't stay there long. My father decided to go north, and my mother didn't want to stay with his family while he was gone. She was pregnant with my brother by then, and she decided to go back to live with her own parents, who had a small farm in Pine Level. They were all alone by then. The niece that they had been raising had married and left. My mother said she thought about the house in Abbeville with a father and mother and growing children, and then she thought about her own mother and father not having anybody with them. So she just up and left and went to stay with her parents.

My mother took me to live with her parents in Pine Level, Alabama, when I was a toddler. Later my father joined us, and we lived as a family until I was two and a half years old. He left Pine Level to find work, and I did not see him again until I was five years old and my brother was three. He stayed several days and left again. I did not see my father anymore until I was an adult and married.

Leona and James McCauley with their daughter Rosa Louise in 1914. Rosa was eighteen months old. (Courtesy of Rosa Parks)

How It All Started

My mother and father never got back together. They just couldn't coordinate their lives together, because he wanted to travel and she wanted to be situated in a permanent home.

My memories of my mother's parents are very clear. In fact, my earliest memory is of my grandfather taking me to the doctor to look at my throat. I had chronic tonsillitis all through my childhood, but this was very early. I wasn't more than about two and a half because it's the only time I can remember being an only child in the house. My mother didn't go. I think she was ailing—it must have been just before my brother was born. My grandfather took me to a store; there wasn't a doctor's office. Grandfather sat me up on the counter, and I remember I was wearing a little red velvet coat and bonnet. The doctor asked me to open my mouth, and I opened it; I can recall that everything the doctor asked me to do, I just obeyed very nicely. The people were amazed, with my being so small and being so little trouble. I opened my mouth, and he put something in it—I thought it was a spoon or something—to hold my tongue down. When Grandfather took me back home, he told my mother and grandmother about how well-behaved I was. That's the first time I can remember anything at all about myself. I always liked to be praised about any little thing. I felt kind of happy because he thought I was such a good little girl.

Living in my grandparents' house, I learned a lot more about my mother's family history. My great-grandfather, my grandmother's father, had the last name of Percival. As a young Scotch-Irish boy he had been brought to the United States on a ship. He was white, but he wasn't free.

In those days, over in Europe, poor white people were sometimes indentured servants. They signed an agreement that in return for their fare to America, they would work for someone for a particular number of years. During those years they had no rights and could be treated as poorly as slaves.

My great-grandfather arrived in this country through the port of Charleston, South Carolina, and then was brought down to Alabama. He was indentured to some people named Wright in Pine Level, but they never changed his name from Percival, which I guess he brought with him from the old country. That was a difference between black slaves and white indentured servants. Black slaves were usually not allowed to keep their names, but were given new names by their owners.

He married Mary Jane Nobles, a person of African descent with no white ancestors. She was a slave and a midwife, who helped to deliver and care for babies. They were married and had three children, two daughters and a son, before freedom was declared by President Abraham Lincoln. Six other children were born free. Their oldest daughter Rose, my grandmother, was five years old when the Civil War ended with a Union victory over the Confederate states.

My grandmother told me that before the Union soldiers arrived, the slave owners had the slaves dig holes and bury many of the slave owners' most valuable household possessions—dishes, silver, and jewelry. The younger slave children were then sent to sit and to play on the freshly dug soil to tamp it down.

After the war ended, slavery was also ended. But many former slaves stayed where they were. They didn't know where else to go and did not want to leave their homes. My great-grandparents stayed on in their small log house on the Wrights' land and continued to work for the family. Life was not very different from before, but they knew they were free to leave if they wanted to. They also had the right to purchase land. I don't know how or when they did it, but some time after Emancipation my great-grandparents purchased twelve acres of land that had been part of the Hudson plantation.

After slavery was ended and the folks found out they were free, that's when my great-grandfather built a little table so his family would have something to eat on. My grandmother was six years old at the time, and the oldest child, and she helped him by holding up a burning pine knot so he could see to work at night. I still use that table today.

During the day my great-grandfather made furniture for Mr. Wright, his former master. I suppose he was using Mr. Wright's tools when he made that little table, or maybe even his own hammer and gimlet. A gimlet is a little tool you use to bore holes in wood. Instead of using nails, he would sharpen a little piece of wood down kind of small and put it in there as a peg. That's how he put the table together.

After Emancipation, my grandmother moved into the house with the Wright family to take care of their child. She wasn't much older than six, but she was large enough to take care of a small child. She didn't have to go out in the fields to work and did not have much work to do around the house either.

My grandfather's father was a white plantation owner named John Edwards, and his mother was a slave housekeeper and seamstress who never went out to work in the fields. I guess she was probably of mixed black and white blood, because my grandfather, the child she had with her owner, was so close to white. She died when my grandfather was very young, and then John Edwards, the plantation owner, died too.

After that, their child, my grandfather Sylvester, was treated very badly. An overseer named Battle took over the plantation, and he disliked my grandfather so much that he beat him every time he saw him. I used to hear my grandfather say that when he was small, the only food he remembered getting was the scraps the kitchen workers would slip to him. The overseer beat him, tried to starve him, wouldn't let him have any shoes, treated him so badly that he had a very intense, passionate hatred for white people. My grandfather was the one who instilled in my mother and her sisters, and in their children, that you don't put up with bad treatment from anybody. It was passed down almost in our genes.

A photo that has been passed down for several generations in Rosa's family, identified as Mary Jane and James Percival. (Courtesy of Rosa Parks)

I remember that he was very emotional and excitable. My grandmother was the calm one. My grandfather was very light complected, with straight hair, and sometimes people took him for white. He took every bit of advantage of being white-looking. He was always doing or saying something that would embarrass or agitate the white people. With those who didn't know him, when he was talking with them he would extend his hand and shake hands with them. He'd be introduced to some white man he didn't know, and he'd say, "Edwards is my name," and shake hands. Then people who knew him would get embarrassed and have to whisper to the others that he was not white. At that time no white man would shake hands with a black man. And black men weren't supposed to introduce themselves by their last names, but only by their first names.

And I remember that sometimes he would call white men by their first names, or their whole names, and not say "Mister." The whites wouldn't always like that too well; in fact, he was taking a big risk. At that time black people were never supposed to call a white person by name without saying "Mister" or "Miss." My grandfather had a somewhat belligerent attitude toward whites in general. And he liked to laugh at whites behind their backs.

My grandfather did not want my brother and me to play with white children. The white overseer of the Hudson plantation had some children just about my age and my brother's age. When we wanted to play with them, or when they wanted to play with us, Grandfather would be very hostile. He made us stay away from them. We wouldn't even have to be close to them. We might be sitting on the ground under the shade of the wagon, playing, and he would yell at us and have us leave from around them.

Any little thing he could do, he did. It wouldn't be anything of great significance, but it was his small way of expressing his hostility toward whites. The whites never did anything to him because of his attitude. How he survived doing all those kinds of things and being so outspoken, talking that big talk, I don't know, unless it was because he was so white and so close to being one of them. I guess they knew him well enough to not bother him physically about it.

His irritability also might have had something to do with his being crippled. He had arthritis. We called it rheumatism then. I don't know how old he was when he became crippled, but I think he was very young. He could hardly wear shoes without cutting holes in the toes, and sometimes he couldn't walk at all. And there he was, trying to take care of a family.

He and my grandmother married very young, and the one thing he wanted most of all was for none of his children or anyone related to him to ever have to cook or clean for whites. He wanted all his children to be educated so they wouldn't have to do that kind of work.

Domestic work paid very little, and those who did domestic work were not respected. Most domestic workers worked very hard and did not have an opportunity to be educated. That's why my grandfather wanted my mother to become educated and teach school. Teaching was a prestigious job, and it paid more. African-American teachers did not receive as much pay as Caucasian teachers, but they were paid more than domestic workers.

My grandfather and grandmother had three daughters. There was one daughter who died in her teens. She never went away from home to school. Another daughter, Fannie, did just what my grandfather didn't want: She left home and went to work in the city of Montgomery in white people's homes. She never went away to school, so that means she never got past the sixth grade, because the black schools around Pine Level didn't go past the sixth grade. For high school you had to go away. She was about seven years older than my mother. Either my grandfather didn't have enough money to send both her and my mother to school or the older one didn't want to go. Most southern women, black or white, didn't go beyond grammar school in those days. I think at one time I heard my mother say that my grandfather had hopes of his oldest daughter being educated, but I guess Fannie had a different idea. Maybe she wanted to make some money right away, even though it was just the little bit of money that housekeepers could make at that time. I think she wanted to be on her own, and she was until she got married. She married before my mother did by several years.

My mother, Leona Edwards, went to school in Selma, Alabama, at Payne University. She didn't go long enough to get a bachelor's degree, but she did get a teaching certificate. She taught in Pine Level, and then of course she met my father and they got married.

After my mother took me back to Pine Level to live with my grandparents, and after my brother, Sylvester, was born, she went back to teaching. The Pine Level black school already had a teacher, so she had to go and teach in the village of Spring Hill. It was too far away for her to walk back and forth every day and still prepare her lessons, so during the week she stayed with a family there. I can remember when she left in the wagon with my grandfather driving. He used a little mule wagon to travel around in. I wasn't exactly sure why she was going away. I said to my grandmother, "Is Mama Leona going to learn how to teach school?" My grandmother said, "No, she's been teaching school since before you were born, so she's just going to teach school." We got that straight, but I was very glad when my mother came back.

I liked being with my grandparents. Sometimes they would take me fishing at a creek on the plantation. Being a little bit up in age, sometimes they couldn't get the bait on the hook, so I used to bait the hooks for them. I guess that's why they liked to take me fishing. I'd get the worm and he could wiggle all he wanted to. All I had to do was get one end of him started on the hook. Some people used to hit the worms and kill them, but I always believed that the fish should see that worm moving on the hook and that they'd bite a lively worm much sooner than a dead one. People used to use other things besides worms too, like fat meat and crawfish tails.

Sylvester, who was named for my mother's father, was two years and seven months younger than I. He followed me around all the time. Whatever I said, he would say it too. He was always getting into mischief, but I was very protective of him. I don't remember this myself, but my grandmother told me that one time when my mother was away, she was going to give my brother a whipping. He was just a little fellow, and she was scolding him, and then she took up a little switch. I said, "Grandma, don't whip brother. He's just a little baby and he doesn't have no mama and no papa either."

And so, she said, she put the switch down and looked at me and decided she would not whip him that day. I can remember what a mischievous little boy he was and how I got more whippings for not telling on things he did than I did for things I did myself. I never did get out of that attitude of trying to be protective of him.

2

Not Just Another Little Girl

Maybe the habit of protecting my little brother helped me learn to protect myself. I do know that I had a very strong sense of what was fair. That attitude got me into trouble sometimes.

One day when I was about ten, I met a little white boy named Franklin on the road. He was about my size, maybe a little bit larger. He said something to me, and he threatened to hit me—balled his fist up as if to give me a sock. I picked up a brick and dared him to hit me. He thought better of the idea and went away.

I didn't think any more of it, and I guess neither did he. But I just happened to mention to my grandmother one morning, "I saw Franklin. He threatened to hit me, and I picked up a brick to hit him." She scolded me very severely about how I had to learn that white folks were white folks and that you just didn't talk to white folks or act that way around white people. You didn't retaliate if they did something to you.

I got very upset about that. I felt that I was very much in my rights to try to defend myself if I could. My grandmother remarked that I was too high-strung and that if I wasn't careful, I would probably be lynched before I was twenty years old. I didn't have any more run-ins with Franklin, but not because I was scared. I just don't remember paying him any attention anymore, though I guess he did pass by. But for me my grandmother's attitude was kind of a hurting thing because I felt that she was taking his side against me. I felt that she was favoring him more than she was me at that time.

Much later I came to understand that my grandmother was scolding me because she was afraid for me. She knew it was dangerous for me to act as if I was just the same as Franklin or anybody else who was white. In the South in those days black people could get beaten or killed for having that attitude.

I didn't have too many other run-ins with white children. Mostly, white children kept to themselves and black children kept to themselves. We went to different schools and different churches and came into contact with each other only once in a while.

My brother and I started school within a year of each other, even though we were more than two years apart in age. I was rather small for my age, and that was one reason why my mother didn't want to send me to school too soon. I was very delicate and had chronic tonsillitis, and my growth had been slowed, actually from the time I was very young. My brother was a larger child than I was, and he and I were always close in size. There were times when we were small that he weighed more than I did. He had eyes that were kind of slanted and he looked almost Oriental. When he was thirteen or fourteen years old, there was a man who used to come by and call him Chink. Sylvester would get terribly angry.

I was about six when I started school. Sylvester started a year later, when he was around five. We went to the one-teacher black school in Pine Level, in a little frame schoolhouse that was just a short distance from where we lived. It was near our church, the Mount Zion A.M.E. Church, right in the churchyard. In many places the church was used as the school, but in Pine Level we had a separate schoolhouse on the church grounds. We had first grade to sixth grade, and there were about fifty to sixty children in the one room. We sat in separate rows by age, and at certain times the larger students would go up to read or recite and then at other times it was the smaller ones' turn.

My first teacher was Miss Sally Hill, and she was very nice. I remember she was a light-brown-skinned lady and she had really large eyes. When the children would tease me or say something to me about how small I was, I would start crying, and I would go up and sit with her. And sometimes she would call me up and talk with me.

I was already reading when I started school. My mother taught me at home. She was really my first teacher. I don't remember when I first started reading, but I must have been three or four. I was very fond of books, and I liked to read and I liked to count. I thought it was something great to be able to take a book and sit down and read, or what I thought was reading. Any books I found where I couldn't read the words, I made up a story about it and talked about the pictures.

At school I liked fairy tales and Mother Goose rhymes. I remember trying to find *Little Red Riding Hood* because someone had said it was a nice book to read. No matter what Miss Hill gave me to read, I would sit down and read the whole book, not just a page or two. And then I would tell her, "I finished this book." Then I started learning to write, making my letters.

I had Miss Hill for only a year. After that Mrs. Beulah McMillan was our teacher. We called her Miss Beulah. She had been a teacher for a long time and had taught my mother when she was a girl. My mother had a picture of this same little school with the students in front of the schoolhouse on the steps—in rows on the steps and down on the ground. The shorter ones and the boys were on their knees on the ground. My mother never wanted me to show it to anybody because it was a real battered-up old picture. But I liked it. I used to take my magnifying glass and look at the faces, which were very small.

I liked Miss Beulah, and I liked school. We had fun there. At recess the girls would play what we called "ring games," like Little Sally Walker Sitting in the Saucer, Rise Sally Rise, and Ring Around the Roses. The boys would play ball. I don't think the girls played much ball at school. We used to play at home a little bit. My mother would buy us a ball, and we'd have to be very careful because pretty soon a rubber ball would be lost. It didn't last too long. We called what we played baseball. I wasn't too active in it, because if I tried to be active I'd fall down and get hurt. I wasn't very good when it came to running sports.

Some of the older boys at school were very good at running sports and playing ball. They were also the ones who were responsible for wood at the school. The larger boys would go out and cut the wood and bring it in. Sometimes a parent would load a wagon up with some wood and bring it to the school, and the boys would unload the wagon and bring the wood inside.

They didn't have to do this at the white school. The town or county took care of heating at the white school. I remember that when I was very young they built a new school for the white children not very far from where we lived, and of course we had to

Black schools in the South were small and crowded. Usually there weren't even desks to work on. (Courtesy of NAACP Public Relations)

pass by it. It was a nice brick building, and it still stands there today. I found out later that it was built with public money, including taxes paid by both whites and blacks. Black people had to build and heat their own schools without the help of the town or county or state.

Another difference between our school and the white school was that we went for only five months while they went for nine months. Many of the black children were needed by their families to plow and plant in the spring and harvest in the fall. Their families were sharecroppers, like my grandparents' neighbors. Sharecroppers worked land owned by plantation owners, and they got to keep a portion of the crop they grew. The rest they had to give to the owner of the plantation. So they needed their children to help. At the time I started school, we went only from late fall to early spring.

I was aware of the big difference between blacks and whites by the time I started school. I had heard my grandfather's stories about how badly he was treated by the white overseer when he was a boy. My mother told me stories the old people had told her about slavery times. I remember she told me that the slaves had to fool the white people into thinking that they were happy. The white people would get angry if the slaves acted unhappy. They would also treat the slaves better if they thought the slaves liked white people.

When white people died, their slaves would have to pretend to be very sorry. The slaves would spit on their fingers and use it to wet their cheeks like it was tears. They'd do this right in front of the little slave children, and then the children would do the same thing in the presence of the grieving white people.

I was glad that I did not live in slavery times. But I knew that conditions of life for my family and me were in some ways not much better than during slavery.

I realized that we went to a different school than the white children and that the school we went to was not as good as theirs. Ours didn't have any glass windows, but instead we had little wooden shutters. Their windows had glass panes.

Some of the white children rode a bus to school. There were no school buses for black children. I remember when we walked to school, sometimes the bus carrying the white children would come by and the white children would throw trash out the windows at us. After a while when we would see the white school bus coming, we would just get off the road and walk in the fields a little bit distant from the road. We didn't have any of what they call "civil rights" back then, so there was no way to protest and nobody to protest to. It was just a matter of survival—like getting off the road—so we could exist from day to day.

Pine Level was too small to have the kind of segregation they had in the cities. I don't know what the ratio of blacks to whites was, but it was a small town. There were very few public facilities, like buses and water fountains, so as a child growing up in Pine Level, I didn't see any drinking fountains marked "Colored" and "White." There was no "downtown." There were just three stores; all basically general stores. All the merchants were white.

There was a post office in one of the stores. There was no railroad depot there, and there wasn't any train nearer than about twelve miles, in a place called Ramer, which was farther west.

By the time I was six, I was old enough to realize that we were actually not free. The Ku Klux Klan was riding through the black community, burning churches, beating up people, killing people. At the time I didn't realize why there was so much Klan activity, but later I learned that it was because African-American soldiers were returning from World War I and acting as if they deserved equal rights because they had served their country.

The whites didn't like blacks having that kind of attitude, so they started doing all kinds of violent things to black people to remind them that they didn't have any rights.

At one point the violence was so bad that my grandfather kept his gun—a double-barreled shotgun—close by at all times. And I remember we talked about how just in case the Klansmen broke into our house, we should go to bed with our clothes on so we would be ready to run if we had to. I can remember my grandfather saying, "I don't know how long I would last if they came breaking in here, but I'm getting the first one who comes through the door."

New members being accepted into the Ku Klux Klan. The white supremacy group did everything it could to intimidate blacks into submission. (The Library of Congress)

We lived right on what they called a highway, which was gravel and not paved at that time. The Klansmen rode on that highway. My grandfather wasn't going outside looking for any trouble, but he was going to defend his home. I remember thinking that whatever happened, I wanted to see it. I wanted to see him shoot that gun. I wasn't going to be caught asleep. I remember that at night he would sit by the fire in his rocking chair and I would sit on the floor right by his chair, and he would have his gun right by just in case.

We were fortunate that the Klansmen never did try to break into our house, and after a while that particular period of violence ended. But there was always violence, and you'd hear about it every time.

I was young and hadn't done much reading about racism, but I did a lot of listening. I heard a lot about black people being found dead and nobody knew what happened. Other people would just pick them up and bury them. Sometimes I'm asked how I lived with that kind of fear, but that was the only way I knew and Pine Level was the only place I knew.

My grandparents were the only black people on that plantation who owned land. They had eighteen acres. Twelve acres were inherited from my great-grandfather James Percival, who purchased the land for himself and his wife, my great-grandmother Mary Jane, after Emancipation and built a small log cabin. The other six acres were given to their daughter, my grandma Rose, to live on as long as she lived. Grandma Rose had taken care of a little girl in the Wright family, who owned the land. When that little girl grew up, she married a merchant from Montgomery named Moses Hudson. The plantation was hers, but after she got married it became known as the Hudson Place. Moses Hudson gave her the land and the house where the Wrights had lived. This is the house we lived in.

On our land we had fruit, pecan, and walnut trees. We maintained a garden and raised chickens and a few cows. We didn't have to buy many things at the stores. My grandfather was the one who usually went to the stores, but sometimes my brother and I would ride in the wagon with him. He would have eggs for sale, and he would trade the eggs for whatever else the family needed but didn't have. He also sold chickens and calves. The stores had most everything we needed, including cloth. I don't remember ever getting any ready-made garments in Pine Level, but we could buy cloth and my mother would sew for us. The little money we earned was from my mother's teaching and from working on other people's land.

When we finished working on our own land, we used to work in Moses Hudson's field. Mr. Sherman Gray was in charge of the field hands. We never called him anything but Mr. Sherman or Mr. Gray, because he was an older man and we respected him. People used to call him the "top nigger." He was half white. He had a big family of children and they lived near us.

I was a field hand when I was quite young—not more than six or seven. I was given a flour sack like the other children and expected to collect one or

Cotton picking was hot, hard work. (Photo by Ben Shahn, courtesy of The Library of Congress)

two pounds of cotton. We would make it a game by seeing who could pick more. When I grew older and stronger, I picked cotton sometimes and chopped cotton at other times.

We picked cotton in the fall of the year after it had matured and was ready to go to the cotton gin. The gin separated the fiber from the cotton seeds. Chopping was done in the spring of the year, when the plants were young. You chopped the weeds from around the plant and sometimes also thinned out the cotton plants so they would grow strong.

We were paid fifty cents per day for chopping cotton and one dollar per hundred pounds of picked cotton. I don't know how much I could pick as a small child, because the children placed their cotton sacks on the ground in the same pile as the adults. Our family put all the cotton we picked together in one pile. When I was ten or twelve years old, my pile was weighed separately.

It was hard work picking and chopping cotton. We had a saying that we worked "from can to can't," which means working from when you can see (sunup) to when you can't (sundown). I never will forget how the sun just burned into me. The hot sand burned our feet whether or not we had our old work shoes on.

Usually we didn't wear shoes. There used to be an expression, "Didn't nobody have shoes on but the hoss [horse] and the boss," and that was how it was for us field hands on the Hudson Place. There were only two sets of good shoes in the field—on Mr. Freeman, the white overseer, and on the horse he rode through the field.

Mr. Freeman was in overall charge. It was his children my grandfather wouldn't let Sylvester and me play with. Mr. Sherman Gray would go up to Mr. Freeman and ask, "What would you all white folks do if you didn't have us niggers to work for you?" suggesting that a compliment was in order for the high-quality work the field hands were doing. Mr. Freeman would answer in an authoritarian manner, "Sherman, if I didn't have you all working for me, I'd have some others. I would have some more damn-fool niggers working." That was exactly what he said. I know, because we were working right there in the field when he said it.

I remember thinking about that and also thinking about another man who was our neighbor. He had a big family of children too, and he was a completely unmixed black man—no white blood at all. He was an older man named Mr. Gus Vaughn. His wife and children worked in the fields, but Mr. Gus Vaughn didn't do anything but walk around on his stick. He didn't work for anybody. He didn't do anything but walk around with his stick and talk big talk. Mr. Freeman couldn't stand Mr. Gus Vaughn. He'd say, "Gus, I don't like you." Mr. Vaughn would answer, "There is no love lost," and just keep walking. I didn't understand what he meant at first, but later I found out that Mr. Gus Vaughn was saying he didn't like Mr. Freeman either—there was no love lost between them.

So I saw that there was at least one black man who wouldn't work for Mr. Freeman. And later on, when I heard white people say that it was the light-skinned black people who had the courage to stand up to whites, I'd always think back and remember Mr. Gus Vaughn who had no white blood.

Not all the white people in Pine Level were hostile to us black people, and I did not grow up feeling that all white people were hateful. When I was very young, I remember, there was an old, old white lady who used to take me fishing. She was real nice and treated us just like anybody else. She used to visit my grandparents a lot, and talk with them for a long time. So there were some good white people in Pine Level.

3

Schooling in Montgomery

Pine Level was my whole world when I was growing up. The first time I went to Montgomery, the nearest big city, I was about eight. My mother kept her teacher's license current by going to summer school at Alabama State Normal, a black teachers' college that is now Alabama State University.

We traveled from Pine Level to Montgomery by car. I don't recall ever in my early years riding a public highway bus. Many years later I remember my husband saying that there was a public bus that ran between Tuskegee and Montgomery (he was living in Tuskegee at one time). But they didn't even let colored people ride inside the bus. They had to sit on top of the bus with the luggage. But growing up in Pine Level, I had never heard of that. If there was a bus, then black people in Pine Level didn't want to put up with that sort of degradation. They preferred to travel by private car.

There were black people in Pine Level who owned cars, and I guess you could say that they had car services. You could pay them to take you where you wanted to go, as long as you were prepared to go when they were ready. Sometimes you would have to get up very, very early in the morning. Some people had trucks, and they would take people places standing up in the back. I don't remember riding in any of the trucks.

We mostly rode with an old man we called Mr. Barefoot. Whenever we got a chance to go into the city, we'd have to be ready early in the morning. He had a little Model T Ford, and he would just fill it up with people.

If you were going to Montgomery to shop, you got off at a little place called Bougahome, which we pronounced "bug-a-home." It was a small business district for farmers, who could purchase staples and feed there. It was the first stop going into Montgomery and the last stop going out of Montgomery.

If you were going to stay in Montgomery, you had to find a place. Black people couldn't stay in the downtown hotels or white boarding houses. There were black boarding houses, but we had to stay with family because my mother's income from teaching was very small. My father had simply disappeared for several years, and he didn't communicate with her very much. If he did write, he sent little money or nothing at all. Also, it was better for women and children to stay with family, and not in the boarding houses.

We stayed with a first cousin of my grandma Rose named Cousin Ida Nobles. My brother, of course, stayed at home with my grandmother and grandfather. He was about six years old. Cousin Ida was a single woman rearing a nephew, her sister's son. Her sister had moved to Chicago and gotten killed by a streetcar. She left this son, who was about sixteen, although I thought he was a grown man, and Cousin Ida had him. But she took a liking to me and wanted me to be her little girl. My mother wanted me to go to school in Montgomery, where I could go nine months of the year. Cousin Ida lived next door to a medical doctor, so if my throat or tonsils hurt, as they did often, medical attention was easily available. My mother thought it was an ideal situation, and she was willing for me to stay with Cousin Ida for the school term. But Cousin Ida wanted to legally adopt me and have me as her own child, change my name and everything. I didn't know about those plans. The grown-ups had me thinking I was just going to be in someone else's care for a while. My mother wasn't willing to give me up, and Cousin Ida wasn't happy about that, so we went to stay with another cousin. I heard about this disagreement only later, when my mother told me. I preferred to stay with my mother. And I did prefer having Sylvester as my younger brother to having Cousin Ida's nephew, whose name was Gus Delaney, for my older brother.

So we left Cousin Ida's house and went to stay with my mother's first cousin, Grandma Rose's nephew. This was one of the Percivals—Cousin Lelar and his wife, Saphonia. They had three young children—Pauline, Claud, and a new baby named Morris. It was my first chance to stay in a house with a new baby, and I enjoyed that. My mother and I stayed with the Percival family until summer school was over, and then we went back to Pine Level.

My mother had me going to school at Alabama State Normal when she was going to school to renew her teaching license. I liked school, and since I was healthier in the summer than in the winter, I did not miss as many days because of illness. The school I attended was a laboratory school where the student teachers could get teaching practice. Alabama Normal seemed like a big school to me compared to my school in Pine Level. There was one big brick building called Tullibody Hall, and there were about four other, smaller buildings. There was an open field with bleachers for sports. I was there only a few weeks before we went back to Pine Level.

I think it was when we got back to Pine Level that I found out they'd stopped having school at Mount Zion and closed up the little frame building. Now we had to go to school at Spring Hill, a church about eight miles away. My mother was the teacher there. She still stayed in Spring Hill during the week.

Sylvester and I walked to and from school every day.

She was a very good teacher. We didn't have a gym, but she believed in exercising. We did stretching exercises to break up the day. We would go outside for that. Indoors she was very creative about doing other things besides reading and writing and studying. We girls did sewing, crocheting, knitting, needleworking. We made baskets out of corn shucks and pine needles. My mother was my teacher until I was eleven. After that she sent me to school in Montgomery.

The school was called the Montgomery Industrial School, but most everyone called it Miss White's school because Miss Alice L. White was the principal and co-founder. The other co-founder was Miss Margaret Beard. Miss White was Caucasian, and so were all the teachers. All the students were African-American girls. My mother sent me there because I couldn't go any further than sixth grade at Spring Hill, and there were no public high schools for blacks in the area. Any black student who wanted to go beyond the sixth grade in public school had to go to Montgomery, to the laboratory school at Alabama Normal.

Now, if I had remained with Cousin Ida, I would have gone to the public junior high school. When I was eight years old, it was called Swayne School. Later it was renamed Booker T. Washington. We used to pass by it, and Cousin Ida would tell me that

that's where I would be going to school if I started living with her. That didn't work out, so my mother had the idea of sending me to Miss White's school because it had a great reputation, better than the public junior high school. My mother wanted me to get the training that Miss White had to offer.

Miss White was from Melrose, Massachusetts. All her faculty were white women from the North. That meant that when they came south to educate black girls, they were ostracized by the white community in Montgomery. Any social life they had, had to be with blacks, and therefore they went to black churches and so on. Miss White had a very rough time. Her school was burned down at least twice in the early days. It had been in existence for quite a number of years when Mother enrolled me there.

Before I started school at Miss White's, I had my tonsils removed in Montgomery. I'd had tonsillitis from the time I was about two years old, and I continued to have severe tonsillitis and had to stay out of school a great deal, especially when the weather turned cool. Out in the country, in the cold and drafty Spring Hill church school, I was always catching a chill. I had colds and sore throats just about all the time.

The doctor I had out in the country had said that my heart was too weak to sustain the general anesthesia that would put me to sleep and that was usually required for the operation. He showed my mother how he could do the operation with me sitting in a chair, and with just a local anesthetic, but she said No. She couldn't stand that. So she went to Montgomery. Her sister Fannie was there, and she had a son, Thomas, who was a few months younger than I was. There wasn't anything wrong with his tonsils at all, or so he said years later when we talked about it. But because my mother and her sister could get both our tonsils removed for the price of one, they went ahead and had us both operated on.

I was very sick after mine were removed. I couldn't see, and my eyes swelled, and my throat didn't heal up very quickly. We were in the hospital one or two nights. It was called Hale's Infirmary, and the doctor was white, as I recall. My mother took me back to Pine Level, and I was sick a long while. My cousin Thomas was up and about in no time. My physical growth increased rapidly after I recovered.

I had no trouble with tonsillitis once my tonsils were removed, but that operation and all the days of school I missed caused me to be put into fifth grade instead of into sixth at Miss White's school. I had already completed the fifth grade at Spring Hill School. But coming out of a rural school, they thought, I might be behind. I remember I was promoted into sixth grade at half term.

My mother paid tuition at Miss White's when I first enrolled there at the age of eleven. I became a scholarship girl later, when it was difficult for Mother to pay the tuition. I would dust the desks, sweep the floor, empty the wastebaskets, and clean the blackboards if the lessons on them were not needed for the following day. I know the school didn't operate just on student tuitions. I think Miss White had some support from the local Presbyterian or Congregational church. She also must have had some Rosenwald support, because I remember when Mr. Julius Rosenwald came to the school one time. We weren't introduced to him, but we knew who he was. He came and observed. I think that was shortly after I arrived.

Mr. Rosenwald was president of Sears, Roebuck & Co., and he was a millionaire. He had a great interest in education, especially the education of black children in the South. Out in the rural areas he built one-room schoolhouses, and people called them Rosenwald schools. My mother used to speak about it. But Miss White's school wasn't any one-room school. It was a three-story building. In fact it's still right there in Montgomery, on Union Street close to High Street. Now it's part of Booker T. Washington High School.

It was separated by a tall board fence from a co-educational Catholic school where all the students were black and all the faculty and religious leaders were white. It seems that there was some animosity between the two schools. And there would have been more than animosity if that tall fence hadn't separated them. Sometimes the Catholic-school kids would climb up and look over the fence, but there wasn't much of that, because Miss White would usually be patrolling around to make sure there were no interchanges between the students—no conversation or bickering.

We usually walked to and from school. Only when the weather was bad did we ride the streetcars. There were no public buses in Montgomery then, just trolleys. These were segregated. When we black people got on, we had to go as far back in the car as we could.

There were other aspects of segregation in Montgomery that I had to get used to. Public water fountains were one. The public water fountains in Montgomery had signs that said "White" and "Colored." Like millions of black children, before me and after me, I wondered if "White" water tasted different from "Colored" water. I wanted to know if "White" water was white and if "Colored" water came in different colors. It took me a while to understand that there was no difference in the water. It had the same color and taste. The difference was who got to drink it from which public fountains.

"Colored" water fountains like this one were the law. (Photo by John Vachon, courtesy of The Library of Congress)

During that time I lived with Aunt Fannie and her children—Howard, Thomas, Annie Mae, and Ella Frances Williamson. Aunt Fannie's husband had died. We lived out from the city a little bit, and there was no way we could get home without going through a white neighborhood. One day my cousin Annie Mae, some other children, and I were walking from school. My cousins went to public school; I was the only one in the family who went to Miss White's school. Anyway, this time we were walking, a white boy was coming along on roller skates, and for some reason he chose me to try and push off the sidewalk. I turned around and pushed him. A white woman was standing not too far from us. She turned out to be his mother, because she said she could put me so far in jail that I never would get out again for pushing her child. So I told her that he had pushed me and that I didn't want to be pushed, seeing that I wasn't bothering him at all.

My mother decided after that incident that it would be better for me to move back with Cousin Lelar and Saphonia Percival. She didn't want me passing through white neighborhoods to get to and from Aunt Fannie's every day. The incident with the white boy on roller skates was the most threatening, but a lot of times white youngsters would approach us and threaten us in some way. We'd have to talk sort of rough to them so that we didn't come to blows.

I liked going to school at Miss White's. It was not hard for me to adjust to being taught by white teachers, because I had learned back in Pine Level, especially from the old woman who used to take me fishing, that white people could treat you like a regular person. There were about 250 to 300 students at the school, and we took the usual classroom subjects, like English and science and

geography. I don't remember having any micro-
scopes in science. If there were any, I didn't use
them. The school wasn't quite that advanced. Anyway, in those days education for young ladies was
mostly home economics.

I think they called it domestic science. They
taught us cooking, sewing, and the care of the sick.
We had a textbook on how to look after patients in
the home, make the beds, feed them, give them
whatever care they needed. In those days, especially
in the South, people didn't go to hospitals that much.
And because most hospitals and doctors were for
whites, most black people were cared for in the
home by black women.

Then the school had what they called occupa-
tional therapy. We made things, including garments. I learned quite a bit about sewing. The older
students had rug weaving. I never got to that.

What I learned best at Miss White's school was
that I was a person with dignity and self-respect,
and I should not set my sights lower than anybody
else just because I was black. We were taught to be
ambitious and to believe that we could do what we
wanted in life. This was not something I learned
just at Miss White's school. I had learned it from
my grandparents and my mother too. But what I
had learned at home was reinforced by the teachers
I had at Miss White's school.

Miss White's school closed after I had been there

about three terms. I remember I had completed the eighth grade. Miss White had become very elderly, and she could no longer maintain the school. She had to give up the job as principal. Most of her faculty were also getting on in years, and it was hard for her to recruit young teachers. None of the teachers at Miss White's felt they could step in and take over the school, and there was no one else to take her place. She'd had a really rough time, and I guess running a school for black girls wasn't a very attractive thing for white people to do. Miss White left the South and went back to Massachusetts, where she died a few years later. I remember getting a letter from her after she went back to the North.

I went to a Miss White's school reunion in 1985. There aren't many of us left. Miss White's former students in Montgomery have placed photographs of her and Miss Beard in the State Archives, so they are honored now while they were ostracized back then.

I was lucky that by the time Miss White's school closed, there was a public junior high school for blacks in Montgomery. Before that time, you could only go through elementary school. There were no public high schools for blacks in Montgomery. You had to go to Birmingham to attend high school unless you enrolled at the laboratory school of Alabama Normal. But they had changed the Swayne

School to Booker T. Washington Junior High, and that's where I went for ninth grade.

By the time I started at Booker T. Washington Junior High, Aunt Fannie had moved to a black neighborhood, so I moved back in with her. Aunt Fannie did cleaning at the Jewish country club—I don't remember the name of it—we just called it the Jews' club. She used to be in very poor health; she was very thin and wasn't able to do much work. So she would take us children to do some of the work for her. The club was in a white community, and there was a vacant lot near the club.

One day her daughter Annie Mae and I were picking berries in the lot. There were white homes nearby. A little boy was looking at us, and he said, "You niggers better leave them berries alone." So she and I started at him, telling him what we would do to him. There was a fence separating us from him, but we said, "If you come over here, we'll give you a good beating." Later we were telling Aunt Fannie about the little boy who got after us about picking berries and what we told him. She said, "You all crazy? You keep your mouths shut. If he'd gone and told somebody, they would have had y'all lynched and all we could do was cry a little bit about it." So that was my second lesson on not talking back to white people. This incident didn't bother me as much as the first one did, because Annie Mae and I were together.

Then there was another time. We lived close to some woods, and there was a creek and we were walking through the woods picking up sticks to take back to the house for firewood. My brother was with us at that time, going to school in Montgomery. A crowd of white boys, in their teens, got after us and threatened to throw my brother in the creek. He wasn't as large as they were, but they were talking about throwing this "big nigger" into the creek. I got after them, saying, "Well you won't be putting nobody in the water unless all of us go in together." So they backed down after they started thinking about us pulling them in after us.

I don't know if it was the same group of white boys or not, but another time my brother said that he and one of his friends were somewhere and the white boys were throwing rocks at them. So they threw some rocks back, and they hit one of the boys and all the white boys left. They soon came back with a man, maybe one of their fathers, and my brother said that the man came with his pistol and he asked the little white boy if my brother and his friend were the same ones who had thrown the rocks. My brother said he never knew why, but the little boy said, "No, they're not the same ones." Perhaps the little boy didn't want to admit who had hit him. Or maybe he didn't want the black boys to be shot. My brother was about thirteen or fourteen years old. That was a very close call for him. He never did mention it at all until we were talking one time after we were grown.

Those run-ins with white children were kind of common, but some of them stand out more than others. A lot of them you forget about, especially when it was only the little smart talk that they'd do. It wasn't that the white children meant to be as cruel as they were, but they had been indoctrinated with that type of attitude by the adults around them.

For grades ten and eleven I went to the laboratory school at Alabama Normal School. By that time it was called Alabama State Teachers' College for Negroes—Negro was the polite, preferred word for black people then. There was still no public high school for blacks in Montgomery. The City of Montgomery did not provide a black high school until 1938, and it was not until 1946 that the black high school had its own building. It was possible for black students to attend the laboratory high school at Alabama State as part of a program for training black teachers. I was there until the eleventh grade. I started the eleventh grade in September, but my grandmother was sick, and I dropped out of high school after about a month to take care of her. She died about a month later. I was sixteen.

After that I returned to Montgomery and I got my first "public" job. Before that time I had done domestic work, cleaning people's houses, from time to time. This job was in a shirt factory, where they made men's blue-denim work shirts. I went back to school at Alabama State for a short time, but then my mother was too sick for me to stay in. She suffered from migraine headaches and swelling of the legs and feet, so I dropped out of school and took care of her while my brother, Sylvester, went to work.

I was not happy about dropping out of school either time, but it was my responsibility to help with my grandmother and later to take care of my mother. I did not complain; it was just something that had to be done.

After my mother got better, I did occasional domestic work, but I mainly took care of the farm until my marriage. I didn't even finish school until after I was married.

4

Marriage, and Activism

I first met Raymond Parks when a mutual friend, a lady I knew very well, introduced us. It seems he had just broken up with a young lady that my friend knew real well, and then she told him that she would like for him to meet me. But I wasn't very interested at that particular time because I'd had some unhappy romantic experiences too.

When he saw me, he wanted to come and call on me, but I thought he was too white. I had an aversion to white men, with the exception of my grandfather, and Raymond Parks was very light skinned. He was in his late twenties and working as a barber in a black barbershop in downtown Montgomery owned by Mr. O. L. Campbell. I was in my late teens. I knew he was interested in me, but I just spoke politely to him and didn't give him another thought.

Later he decided to look me up again. He came driving down our road and he saw my mother standing on the porch. He'd already asked an elderly lady farther down the road if she knew me. People couldn't imagine what a person like him was doing around there asking questions; they thought he was a white man. So the first person he asked did not acknowledge knowing me.

Farther on down the road he saw my mother standing on the porch with her hair in braids, and he stopped to speak to her. He asked if she knew where I lived, and of course she turned out to be my mother, and she invited him in, and that's when we got acquainted. He came in and sat down and talked a little while. I was very shy and still wasn't interested in him. He came back, and this time I wouldn't go out to see him. I went to bed and covered up and wouldn't come out. I heard him say, "If she's gone to bed, I won't stay," and off he went.

But he came back again, and after that we started going on rides to different places. He had a car, a little red Nash with a rumble seat in the back. It was something very special for a young black man to own his own car, particularly when he wasn't driving for any of the white folks. We young people used to sit in the rumble seats and get rides from some of the fellows when they were driving white people's cars (unbeknown to the white people, of course).

Parks—everyone called him Parks—was a very nice person, and I enjoyed talking to him. He would drive along and tell me about his life experiences and problems that he'd had as a youngster growing up and being very fair complected.

He was born on the 12th of February in 1903, the same month I was born, in a place called Wedowee, Alabama, near Roanoke in Randolph County, northeast of Montgomery. His parents were David Parks and Geri Culbertson Parks. Both his parents had died by the time we met. His father had left his mother when Raymond was an infant, and he never saw him again. His father died from a fall off a house roof while he was working as a carpenter.

He told me he grew up in an all-white neighborhood, completely surrounded by white people. Parks was so light, he could have passed for white, but he didn't have white people's hair. He was the only black child in the neighborhood, and they wouldn't let him go to the neighborhood school because it was a white school. He didn't live near enough to the black school to go there, so his mother taught him to read and write as a young child at home. He attended school briefly in Roanoke, Alabama, when he was a young man. Aside from that he didn't have any formal schooling.

Parks looked after his ill mother and grandmother until they died when he was in his late teens. Then he got a job as a sexton at a white Baptist church in Roanoke. He took care of the church and the church grounds. They had just bought some shrubbery to put around the church, and Parks was supposed to water it, which he did. He didn't water it in the middle of the day, but in the evening after the sun went down. The wife of one of the deacons told the pastor that he had not watered the shrubbery.

The pastor spoke to him about it, saying, "Mrs. Jones told me you didn't water the shrubbery." Parks said he did. The pastor said, "Mrs. Jones told me you didn't water it, and if her husband knows you dispute her word, he will sweep up this churchyard with you." Parks said he told the pastor he did water the shrubbery. He said, "I didn't water it in the middle of the day but when I was supposed to, to keep the sun from scorching it. And Mr. and Mrs. Jones will not wipe up the churchyard with me and neither will you." He told me that the reason he could say that was because he had a pistol in his pocket, and in case he had to, he could use it.

Parks said he always did his best to get along, but whenever white people accosted him, he always wanted to let them know he could take care of business if he had to. They didn't bother you so much back then if you just spoke right up. But as soon as you acted like you were afraid, they'd have fun with you.

Parks left home after that. He had a very young sister at home, but he asked one of his cousins to take care of her. He said that he couldn't stay there anymore and that he never did like to be around white folks too much because he would just have to give them "sass." White folks used to say you were sassy if you spoke right up to them.

Parks was in his early twenties when he left home. After that he had several jobs and moved around quite a bit. He spent some time in Tuskegee, where he learned barbering. By the time I met him, he was twenty-eight and living in Montgomery and working as a barber. He was the first man of our race, aside from my grandfather, with whom I actually discussed anything about the racial conditions. And he was the first, aside from my grandfather and Mr. Gus Vaughn, who was never actually afraid of white people. So many African Americans felt that you just had to be under Mr. Charlie's heel—that's what we called the white man, Mr. Charlie—and couldn't do anything to cross him. In other words Parks believed in being a man and expected to be treated as a man.

I was very impressed by the fact that he didn't seem to have that meek attitude—what we called an "Uncle Tom" attitude—toward white people. I thought he was a very nice man, an interesting man who talked very intelligently. He could talk for hours at a time about all the things he had lived through.

Parks was also the first real activist I ever met.

He was a long-time member of the NAACP, the National Association for the Advancement of Colored People, when I met him. It was the spring of 1931 when we got to know each other, and the Scottsboro case had come up. Parks was the first person ever to mention that case to me—about what was going on with the Scottsboro Boys and how he and a few others had gotten together to raise money to help pay for the legal fees and defend them in court and keep them out of the electric chair. They were working in secret, and he didn't even tell me the names of the others. Parks used to say that all their names were Larry.

The Scottsboro Boys were nine young men who didn't even know each other before they were arrested on charges of raping two white women. Haywood Patterson, Eugene Williams, and brothers Roy and Andy Wright were from Chattanooga, Tennessee. Clarence Norris, Charlie Weems, Olen Montgomery, Ozie Powell, and Willie Roberson were from various parts of Georgia. They ranged in age from nineteen down to fourteen. They were all hoboing on the same freight train that went from Tennessee through Georgia to Alabama. There were many others on that freight train, African American and Caucasian. It was the time of the Great Depression, and millions of people were out of work. A lot of them rode the trains looking for jobs. At some point the whites on that particular train started throwing

Seven of the Scottsboro Boys are led handcuffed from Morgan County Jail to the courtroom in November 1933. (AP/Wide World Photo)

gravel at the blacks and telling them to get off the train. The blacks fought back and threw most of their attackers off the train near Stevenson, Alabama.

Farther on the train stopped to take on water at Paint Rock, Alabama. A white mob was waiting, armed with sticks and guns, and they forced the blacks off the train and threatened to lynch them.

61

But the police came along and broke up the mob. Then they put handcuffs on the young black men and took them to the nearest jail, in Scottsboro, Alabama. That is why the young men came to be called the Scottsboro Boys. The police also put the white hobos in jail.

The next day the police took the blacks from the holding pen where they had spent the night and lined them up in front of two white women, Ruby Bates and Victoria Price. Ruby Bates picked out six of them and claimed they had raped her. The police decided that it stood to reason that the other three had raped Victoria Price, although she hadn't picked them out.

The defendants went to trial on April 6, 1931. The Interdenominational Ministers' Alliance, a group of black preachers in Chattanooga, Tennessee, raised $50.00 to pay a lawyer. He met with the young men for one half hour before the trial. There were four trials for the nine defendants, and all together the trials lasted three days. The two women testified that the defendants had beat them and used guns and knives, but the police hadn't found any guns or knives. Two doctors testified that the women did not have any wounds or bruises. But the judge made it clear that he thought the defendants were guilty and that the trials were a waste of time and money. All were found guilty. On April 9 the judge sentenced all but the youngest to die in the electric chair on July 10.

I thought it was awful that they were condemned to die for a crime they did not commit. It demonstrated how little regard segregationists had for the lives of black people and the lengths they would go to, to keep us in fear.

By this time the case had made the newspapers, and people outside the South were up in arms about the way the young men had been railroaded. By the end of April the International Labor Defense, a Communist organization, had stepped in to help them. By early May the NAACP was on the case. Between them these two organizations managed to get the execution date set aside and filed an appeal. In November the United States Supreme Court ordered a new trial for the defendants on the grounds that the lawyer at the first trials did not really represent them. The trials and appeals went on for years and years. Not until 1950 was the last defendant released on parole.

Parks was working for the Scottsboro Boys from the beginning. I don't know if he was working officially with one of the big organizations. The people he was working with came from places other than Montgomery. He was working with them when I first met him, and then through that year and the next year he was still involved. Whites accused anybody who was working for black people of being a Communist, but I don't think anyone in Parks' group was a Communist.

I was proud of Parks for working on behalf of the Scottsboro Boys. I also admired his courage. He could have been beaten or killed for what he was doing. Later I came to understand that he was always interested in and willing to work for things that would improve life for his race, his family, and himself.

The second time Parks and I were ever in each other's company, he talked about getting married. I hadn't given marriage a thought at all. He spoke about it, and I didn't pay it any attention. But one day he said, "I really think we ought to get married," and I agreed with him. The next day, when I was at church, he asked my mother's permission to marry me, and when I came home from church she told me that she had agreed. He didn't actually propose to me at all, or anyway not formally.

That was in August of 1932. We were married in December of 1932 in Pine Level, in my mother's home. It was not a big wedding, just family and close friends. We didn't even send out any invitations. After we got married, we went to live on the east side of Montgomery not very far from Alabama State, in a rooming house on South Jackson Street that was owned by some people named Quarterman.

My husband was very supportive of my desire to finish school, and I went back to school after we were married. I received my high school diploma in 1933 when I was twenty years old. At that time only a small percentage of black people in Montgomery were high school graduates. In 1940, seven years after I got my diploma, only seven out of every hundred had as much as a high school education.

But that still didn't help me much in getting a job. I had a high school diploma, but I could only get jobs that didn't need a high school diploma. I worked as a helper at St. Margaret's Hospital. I took in sewing on the side.

In 1941 I got a job at Maxwell Field, the local Army Air Force base. The base was integrated because President Roosevelt had issued an order forbidding segregation in the public places, trolleys, or buses at military bases.

I could ride on an integrated trolley on the base, but when I left the base, I had to ride home on a segregated bus. I remember there was a white woman who lived in the same building on the base where I worked. We would get on the base bus and sit right across from each other. She had a little boy about nine years old. She and the little boy would be sitting together, and this other worker named Rose and I would be sitting together, and we'd sit across from each other and talk. And then when we'd get the city bus, the white woman would stop at the front and we'd go to the back and the little boy would be looking at us so strangely. That woman was from Mississippi, but it didn't bother her to ride with us.

Sometimes on the base there were problems with individuals. I did not experience any unpleasant incidents, but years later my husband got a job at the barber shop on the base, which was a private concession. I remember Parks telling me about going to the cafeteria and sitting down at one end of a long table. Two white women came in and sat down at the other end, and this white man got after him for sitting at the same table with them. But that was not the fault of the Army Air Force base, that was just this particular man.

Parks kept going to his night meetings about the Scottsboro case. I didn't go to the meetings because it was very dangerous. Whenever they met, they had someone posted as lookout, and someone always had a gun. That was something that he didn't want me to take an active part in, because the little committee he was working with had to meet late at night and into the morning when everybody else was asleep. He didn't want me to go because it was hard enough if he suddenly had to run. He wouldn't be able to leave me, and I couldn't run as fast as he could. Also, he felt that I was just too young at the time.

He also did not tell me much about what went on at those meetings. That way if someone asked me, I could truthfully say I didn't know. He wanted to protect me.

I remember a meeting we had when we were living on Huffman Street in what they called a shotgun house. You could shoot one bullet and it would go through the whole house because of the way the rooms were lined up one behind the other. It was the first meeting we'd ever had at our house, and it was in the front room. There was a little table about the size of a card table that they were sitting around. This was the first time I'd seen so few men with so many guns. The table was covered with guns. I didn't even think to offer them anything—refreshments or something to drink. But with the table so covered with guns, I don't know where I would have put any refreshments. No one was thinking of food anyway.

I can remember sitting on the back porch with my feet on the top step and putting my head down on my knees, and I didn't move throughout the whole meeting. I just sat there. I guess there were about half a dozen men. I can't even remember who they were, although I probably knew them. After the meeting was over, I remember, my husband took me by the shoulders and kind of lifted me from the porch floor. I was very, very depressed about the fact that black men could not hold a meeting without fear of bodily injury or death. Also I was reminded of the time I was a child and I sat next to my grandfather waiting for the Ku Klux Klan to ride down on us.

There were never any women at those meetings. I don't think the men barred women; it was just that it was so dangerous. There was a woman my husband talked about—he called her Captola. She was involved somehow, but she didn't go to the meetings. Not many men were activists in those days either, because if it was known that they were meeting, they would be wiped right out. But it didn't bother me being married to Parks. He was doing the same thing before we got married; and I knew how dangerous it was.

There was one white woman who helped them. She never came to our house, but Parks and I went to her house at one time. She saw that Parks and his friends had money when they needed it. At other times they would take up collections of nickels and dimes or whatever they could get to pay the lawyer.

After a while we left Huffman Street and moved to South Union Street, where we stayed with Mr. King Kelly, who was a deacon of the Dexter Avenue Baptist Church. Mr. Kelly and his wife were very much against the type of thing Parks was doing. Mr. King Kelly had worked for the Capitol Clothing Store, a men's clothing store in Montgomery, for a long long time as a man of all work, and I guess he was afraid of losing his job. So Parks never held any meetings at the Kelly house.

During the time when the Scottsboro case was in all the newspapers, the police were always on the lookout for people to intimidate. They'd try to find out where the people who were doing this late-night meeting lived and who they were. One night two cops on motorcycles passed by. I was sitting on the porch on the swing, and Mr. Kelly was on the porch too. I kept talking about how a couple of days before, the police had killed two men who were connected with the group Parks was with, people Parks knew well. Every time he was at those meetings with those people, I wondered if he would come back alive, if he wouldn't be killed.

So I was there on the porch on the swing, and the two motorcycle cops were going up and down the same block. They would go down and turn around and come back. I was so frightened, I was shaking. Later Mr. Kelly said, "I could hear that swing trembling while you were sitting there." I didn't even realize I was shaking so much that I was making the swing tremble.

When Parks came home, he knew the cops were out there. So instead of coming in the front door as usual, he came up from the back. There was a little pathway back to Bainbridge Street from where we lived, and he came through there and in the back door. Next thing I knew, he was in the house. So I felt better. At least they didn't get him that time.

While we were living at Mr. Kelly's, an incident happened to me that I didn't even tell my husband about. I went downtown to the railroad station with the Kellys—Mr. Kelly and his daughter and her two children—to see them off on the train. I was walking a little behind them. We were on our way to the train when a policeman approached me and asked if I had a ticket. I told him, "No." He pushed me back against the railing and said, "If you don't have a ticket, you can't go." I knew that he had a club and a gun and that there wasn't anything for me to do but just get out of the way. It upset me quite a bit.

What really upset me was that another young black woman was there—about my age, early twenties. I guess she must have been somebody who knew the policeman, because she was kind of playing with him, saying, "I'm going through." He said, "No, don't you go through," and he sort of swung his club in her direction. She laughed, and that upset me just as much, because she seemed rather familiar with him.

To me, she showed a lack of respect for herself as a woman, and especially as a black woman. She had seen him treat me with disrespect. His treatment of her was just as disrespectful, but she had laughed about it.

Mr. Kelly came back and wanted to know why I hadn't gone with them. I just said, "The policeman wouldn't let me go." I didn't tell him what had happened. I didn't tell my husband either, because he would have been very upset about it.

5

We Fight for the Right to Vote

After the Scottsboro Boys were saved from execution, Parks got involved in voter registration, which was something he was interested in even before we met. He was very discouraged about how few blacks were registered to vote.

The right to vote is so important for Americans. We vote for people to represent us in government. If we do not like the way they represent us, we can vote for someone else. But in those days most black people in the South could not vote.

The segregationists made it very difficult for black people to register to vote. In order to get registered, blacks had to have white people to vouch for them. A small number of blacks who were in good favor with the white folks did get registered in that way. But once they got registered, they did not want other blacks to do the same. I guess they felt that when the white people vouched for and approved of them being registered, that put them on a different level from the rest of us. They would tell Parks and his friends that they ought to go about their business and not be concerned about registration and voting.

That's how it was in those days. Most blacks were afraid. Those who were in good favor with the white folks didn't want to lose their privileged position. The rest didn't think anything could be done. There really wasn't any activist, public civil-rights movement that masses of people participated in until the Montgomery bus boycott in 1955. Until then only a few people were activists, and of course they were *not* in good favor with the whites.

My husband never did get registered in Alabama. He tried for a long time, but he never would agree to go even with some of his white acquaintances who said they would vouch for him. He wanted to get registered on his own. The first time he ever registered was years later, when we were living in Detroit, Michigan. In Montgomery in the 1940s we had what we called a Voters' League, a group of people who had meetings in each other's homes, mostly in our house. At that time I had a list of the black registered voters in Montgomery. There were thirty-one people on the registered list, and some of them were in the cemetery. They had died but they were still on the list. So there were very few, and we didn't get much accomplished until Mr. E. D. Nixon decided to break down those barriers.

Mr. Edgar Daniel Nixon was one of the most active African Americans in Montgomery. He was a railroad porter and president of the local branch of the Brotherhood of Sleeping Car Porters, which was a black railroad workers' union founded by Mr. A. Philip Randolph. Mr. Nixon had founded the Montgomery branch of the Brotherhood of Sleeping Car Porters back in the 1920s. When I first met him in 1943, he was president of the Montgomery Branch of the National Association for the Advancement of Colored People. He was a proud, dignified man who carried himself straight as an arrow. In getting black people registered to vote, he had the help of a black lawyer named Arthur A. Madison, a native of Alabama who was practicing in New York City. Mr. Madison came down for a while and worked with quite a few of us, giving us instructions on getting registered. He said there was no need for us to have to wait until some white person approved of us and took us down to the registration office to vouch for us. He also told us about the test we would have to take, which was called a literacy test, to see if we could read and write and understand the U.S. Constitution. He was arrested and jailed for trying to help us, and later returned to New York.

I decided to get registered. The first year I tried was 1943. They would open the registration books only at a certain time. If you didn't know when that was, you missed your chance. They didn't make any public announcements. You had to call and find out. And then they might decide to have registration on a Wednesday morning from ten o'clock until noon, when they knew most black working people couldn't get there. Even if you took off from work to be there, it didn't mean you would get to register. If noon-time came, they would close the doors, no matter how many people were still standing in line. All this was to keep African Americans from being able to register.

Even if you got inside, you couldn't necessarily be registered. It used to be that you needed to own property, but by the time I tried to register, they said, "You should have property, but if you can pass the test by answering the questions correctly, you don't have to own property." So you either had to own property or pass the test.

The first day in 1943 that was selected for registration was a working day for me, so I couldn't go. Mr. Nixon and, I'm sure, Attorney Madison were able to pass the word to the black community, so a long line of black people formed around the courthouse waiting to register. My mother and my cousin were a part of that group. They, along with many others, received their voter's certificates in the mail. Certificates were mailed to African Americans, while Caucasians received them immediately after completing the test.

The following day, which was my day off, I went down to register and take my test, but I did not receive a certificate in the mail.

The second time I tried, I was denied. They just told me, "You didn't pass." They didn't have to give you a reason. I thought I had passed the test, but I had no way of knowing. They could say you didn't pass the test and there would be nothing you could do about it. The registrars could do whatever they wanted to do.

I was pretty sure I had passed the test. So, the third time I took the test, in 1945, I made a copy of my answers to those twenty-one questions. They didn't have copy machines in those days. I copied them out by hand. I was going to keep that copy and use it to bring suit against the voter-registration board. But I received my certificate in the mail. I was finally a registered voter. The next thing I had to do was to pay my accumulated poll tax.

The poll tax was $1.50 a year, and every registered voter had to pay it. But it was mostly black people who had to pay it retroactive. They didn't deny the right to vote to whites; so the white person, when he was twenty-one years old (you couldn't vote at eighteen at that time), could go in and get registered and just pay the $1.50 a year from then on. If you were older and registered, you had to pay the poll tax back to the time you were twenty-one. I got registered in 1945 when I was thirty-two years old, so I had to pay $1.50 for each of the eleven years between the time I was twenty-one and the time I was thirty-two. At that time $16.50 was a considerable amount of money.

If I had brought suit against the voter-registration people, I would have had to get someone to represent me. And in the beginning there was no black lawyer in Montgomery I could call on. In fact, there were very few black lawyers practicing in Alabama at that time. The only lawyer we could call on when we needed to was Arthur D. Shores of Birmingham. He would occasionally come down. I knew he had represented William P. Mitchell and some others who wanted to get registered in Macon County. But by this time we had the help of Arthur A. Madison. I remember going down to the polling place with Mr. Nixon and Attorney Madison. But that time I did get registered, so I didn't have to bring a lawsuit.

I remember the first election for governor that I voted in. I voted for Jim Folsom, who was running against a very reactionary and very racist man named Handy Ellis. There were no unpleasant incidents, and I felt that I had gone through an awful lot of trouble to do something so simple and uneventful.

The second time I tried to register to vote, I was put off a Montgomery city bus for the first time. I didn't follow the rules.

Black people had special rules to follow. Some drivers made black passengers step in the front door and pay their fare, and then we had to get off and go around to the back door and get on. Often, before the black passengers got around to the back door, the bus would take off without them. There were thirty-six seats on a Montgomery bus. The first ten were reserved for whites, even if there were no white passengers on the bus. There was no law about the ten seats in the back of the bus, but it was sort of understood that they were for black people. Blacks were required to sit in the back of the bus, and even if there were empty seats in the front, we couldn't sit in them. Once the seats in the back were filled, then all the other black passengers had to stand. If whites filled up the front section, some drivers would demand that blacks give up their seats in the back section.

It was up to the bus drivers, if they chose, to adjust the seating in the middle sixteen seats. They carried guns and had what they called police power to rearrange the seating and enforce all the other rules of segregation on the buses. Some bus drivers were meaner than others. Not all of them were hateful, but segregation itself is vicious, and to my mind there was no way you could make segregation decent or nice or acceptable.

The driver who put me off was a mean one. He was tall and thickset with an intimidating posture.

His skin was rough-looking, and he had a mole near his mouth. He just treated everybody black badly. I had been on his bus as a passenger before, and I remember when a young woman got on the bus at the front and started to the back and he made her get off the bus and go around to the back door. One day in the winter of 1943 the bus came along, and the back was crowded with black people. They were even standing on the steps leading up from the back door. But up front there were vacant seats right up to the very front seats. So I got on at the front and went through this little bunch of folks standing in the back, and I looked toward the front and saw the driver standing there and looking at me. He told me to get off the bus and go to the back door and get on. I told him I was already on the bus and didn't see the need of getting off and getting back on when people were standing in the stepwell, and how was I going to squeeze on anyway? So he told me if I couldn't go through the back door that I would have to get off the bus—"my bus," he called it. I stood where I was. He came back and he took my coat sleeve; not my arm, just my coat sleeve.

He didn't take his gun out. I was hardly worth the effort because I wasn't resisting. I just didn't get off and go around like he told me. So after he took my coat sleeve, I went up to the front, and I dropped my purse. Rather than stoop or bend over to get it,

I sat right down in the front seat and from a sitting position I picked up my purse.

He was standing over me and he said, "Get off my bus." I said, "I will get off." He looked like he was ready to hit me. I said, "I know one thing. You better not hit me." He didn't strike me. I got off, and I heard someone mumble from the back, "How come she don't go around and get in the back?"

I guess the black people were getting tired because they wanted to get home and they were standing in the back and were tired of standing up. I do know they were mumbling and grumbling as I went up there to get myself off the bus. "She ought to go around the back and get on." They always wondered why you didn't want to be like the rest of the black people. That was the 1940s, when people took a lot without fighting back.

I did not get back on the bus through the rear door. I was coming from work, and so I had already gotten a transfer slip to give the next driver. I never wanted to be on that man's bus again. After that, I made a point of looking at who was driving the bus before I got on. I didn't want any more run-ins with that mean one.

6

Secretary of the NAACP

By the time I was put off the bus, I was a member of the NAACP. It was a national organization with headquarters in New York, founded by a small group of African Americans and Caucasians who believed in democracy. They chose February 12, 1909, to start the organization, in honor of President Abraham Lincoln's birthday. They formed the group to protest against racial discrimination, lynching, brutality, and unequal education.

In Alabama, in the early 1940s, there were a few local branches—in Montgomery, Birmingham, and Mobile. Parks was a member of the Montgomery branch, but he did not encourage me to join because he felt it was too dangerous. Members of the Montgomery NAACP risked reprisals for being activists. I did not know there were any women involved until I saw in the *Alabama Tribune* a picture of Johnnie Carr, my friend and classmate at Miss White's school. She was the only female member, and there was no youth division of the branch.

The article said that Johnnie was working with the Montgomery branch of the NAACP, in fact I think she was secretary at that time. So I thought, Maybe one time I'll go over to the NAACP and see if I can run into Johnnie. In December of 1943 they were having their annual election of officers meeting, and I went to it. That day she wasn't at the meeting, and there were just a few men, maybe about a dozen or fifteen. I paid my membership dues, and then they had the election of officers. I was the only woman there, and they said they needed a secretary, and I was too timid to say no. I just started taking minutes, and that was the way I was elected secretary. There was no pay, but I enjoyed the work, and Parks was very supportive of my involvement.

Going back to the late 1930s, or even earlier, and into the late 1940s, I really didn't know of that many women who were involved in civil-rights work. Of course, I wasn't that involved myself, being rather young. But by the time you got to the late 40s and even into the 50s and 60s, women became more vocal and active. More tried to get registered to vote and went to voters' meetings.

I remember when I first joined the NAACP and became the secretary, the only two women who attended the meetings were Johnnie Carr and me. Mr. E. D. Nixon was president then, and once in a while

The Montgomery NAACP, 1953–54. Rosa is at right; her mother is two seats behind her; Mr. E. D. Nixon is the first in the middle row; Johnnie Carr is two seats behind him. (Courtesy of Rosa Parks)

Mrs. Nixon would come to a meeting, but I think she just kept up with the meetings because he was always on the scene. I remember I would be working hard trying to get articles out for Mr. Nixon, sending letters, and going to meetings, and he would just laugh. He used to say, "Women don't need to be nowhere but in the kitchen."

I would ask him, "Well, what about me?" He would respond, "But I need a secretary and you are a good one." He always complimented my work and encouraged me to continue.

Most of the members of the Montgomery NAACP were black. White people had to have a lot of courage to join, because they would be ostracized by the white community. It was still very dangerous for anyone, black or white, to try to help black people. We got more help from northern whites. I remember the time when Andy Wright, one of the Scottsboro Boys, was in trouble because he had violated his parole by going out of the state of Alabama. I think he went into the state of Tennessee to visit his mother. He was rearrested in August of 1946, and the parole board didn't restore his freedom until June of 1947. Later he was rearrested and returned to prison, and then he was again set free on parole. There was a Mrs. Zenobia Johnson who was on a committee in defense of Andy Wright. She was black. She and her husband were in charge of the dining room at Alabama State, where I was in the laboratory school for high school. Mrs. Johnson, along with four other members—Mr. W. G. Porter, Professor J. E. Pierce, Mr. E. D. Nixon, and I—made up the defense committee. We met with the all-white parole board to support Andy Wright.

A woman on the parole board suggested that Andy and the other Scottsboro Boys were not treated badly in prison because they had received money from northern sympathizers. She referred to them as being "pampered." The committee maintained that the Scottsboro Boys were imprisoned unjustly, and that if they were freed, they would not require "pampering."

The parole board did vote in favor of parole for Andy. Our branch of the NAACP helped him get a job driving a truck, and we kept in touch with him.

As secretary of the NAACP, I recorded and sent membership payments to the national office, answered telephones, wrote letters, and sent out press releases to the newspapers. One of my main duties was to keep a record of cases of discrimination or unfair treatment or acts of violence against black people.

There were many, many cases to keep records on. I remember one case out in Abbeville, Alabama, where my father and his family came from. Mrs. Recy Taylor of Abbeville, a black woman, was on her way home from church when she was kidnapped—forced into a car at gun- and knifepoint—stripped of her clothing, and raped by six white men on September 3, 1944. A Henry County grand jury refused to indict the six white men, although the driver of the kidnap car confessed and named his accomplices. A lot of people, blacks and whites, were up in arms about this. Some people formed a Committee for Equal Justice for Mrs. Taylor. Mrs. Caroline Bellin, the white executive secretary of the committee, tried to help Mrs. Taylor and came to Montgomery to the NAACP, since the NAACP didn't have a branch in Abbeville. That was during the summer of 1945.

We tried to help, but there wasn't much we could do. Mrs. Bellin tried to visit Mrs. Taylor's home in Abbeville, but the sheriff manhandled her and ordered her to stay out of the Negro section of town. The NAACP and the committee managed to get Governor Chauncey Sparks to convene a special grand jury to investigate the case, but that special grand jury also refused to indict the men.

Of course, the opposite was true if a white woman cried rape and accused a black man. The things that young black men suffered because of white women! I remember poor Jeremiah Reeves. He was a delivery driver, just a teenager. A white woman used to have him come over to her house (they were having an affair), and people began to notice it.

On this particular day a neighbor or somebody peeked through a window and saw them in the act of undressing. As soon as the woman detected someone looking in, she started yelling rape. The police came and caught him. He was seventeen or eighteen years old at the time.

His mother brought the case to the NAACP and

we struggled with it for quite a few years. I was working at Crittenden's Tailor Shop, and I remember discussing the case with my friend and co-worker, Bertha Butler. I said, "I sure wish I knew where that woman lived, so I could go out there and see if she would tell the truth. If there was anybody else who would go with me . . ."

Bertha said, "Girl, you know your mother and husband aren't going to let you go out there." But I was ready to risk it if I could have found someone else to go along with me.

There was never any evidence against Jeremiah Reeves, except that woman's word that he raped her. I tried to find some way of documenting that she'd lied, but I was never able to do so. He was on Death Row for several years. He used to write poetry. Some of it was published, and I read it and saved it. He wrote a lot of poems. His mother, as a young woman, was so beautiful, like a movie star to me. Her maiden name was Cornella Snow. She was married and had several children. Jeremiah was her eldest. We in the Montgomery branch of the NAACP worked for quite a few years to save Jeremiah Reeves, but we couldn't save him. He stayed on Death Row until he was twenty-one, and then they executed him. It was a tragedy that he lost his life. Sometimes it was very difficult to keep going when all our work seemed to be in vain.

Of course once in a while a white woman would not cry rape just to save herself. I remember reading in the daily paper about a case in south Alabama involving a white woman, a widow with a nine-year-old boy. She had a black man friend who visited her. He had a family, so she didn't have him come to the house. She prepared a room in her garage, fixed it up like a bedroom, and that's where they would spend time when he went to see her. Somebody must have become suspicious, because on one of the visits the police came and found them. She refused to say it was rape. She just admitted they were having an affair. She would not let them touch him, just forbade them to touch him, and so they arrested her. There were laws against miscegenation, which means blacks and whites having affairs or marrying. The man left town, with whatever money she could give him because she was well off. She stayed and was ostracized by the town, and I later read that she committed suicide.

It was terribly hard getting people to come forward with what they knew in cases of white violence against blacks. I remember a black minister in Union Springs, Alabama, I once tried to interview. He had seen a white man shoot a black man named Thomas after the white man found out they were both seeing the same black woman. The minister saw the shooting, and he just took off running.

Some people said he ran over everything on the road to get to Montgomery. When he got to Montgomery, he was talking with my husband, and my husband said, "Rosa will talk with you." I got my pen and paper and started to take down his statement, but he couldn't go through with it. He didn't admit that he was frightened, he just said he was away from home and didn't have his family with him and he had to think about so many things.

In order to try and bring any type of charge against the man who committed the murder, we had to have a statement from the only witness. But he would not, or could not, testify or even dictate a statement. At least with a statement we could have had it notarized and sent to the Department of Justice in Washington, D.C. But he couldn't do it.

My husband got upset with the man, because the man wouldn't talk to me. So I said, "Don't be too hard on him." It was very difficult. People didn't have any inclination to give up their lives just to try to bring a charge against somebody else.

There was another case that was very similar. It involved a black man named Elmore Bolling who was reasonably well off. He had a long truck and he would haul cattle. I used to see him driving along the street taking cattle to slaughter. A white man killed him too, and it was for the same reason as in the other case. The white man said it was because Elmore Bolling had insulted his wife over the telephone, and he pleaded self-defense. But the real reason was that he was going with a black woman, and he caught her and Elmore Bolling together.

I used to have notes about all these cases, but I don't have them in my possession now. I kept them at the NAACP office, because I went there all the time. Later on, Mr. Nixon had them stored in a small building on his property, and someone threw them out by mistake. A great deal of history was lost, because we kept notes on many cases. But we didn't have too many successes in getting justice. It was more a matter of trying to challenge the powers that be, and to let it be known that we did not wish to continue being treated as second-class citizens.

7

White Violence Gets Worse

There were more violent incidents against black people in the late 1940s, after World War II ended. Black soldiers who had served in the armed forces were coming home, and they felt as if they should have equal rights since they had served their country.

My brother, Sylvester, had been drafted into the Army in the early 1940s. He had served in both Europe and the Pacific. The armed forces were segregated at that time, and the black soldiers were assigned the less appealing jobs, like maintenance and caring for the severely wounded. Promotions were given very sparingly to black soldiers. In other words, in the armed services, which were controlled by white racists, it was business as usual. But people in England and France received the African-American soldiers warmly. Many of these soldiers had white girlfriends, and some even married English or French or Italian women. The soldiers

Black soldiers fought hard for their country during World War II, but were rewarded with racism when they returned to the South. (Courtesy of NAACP Public Relations)

felt appreciated for what they were doing in the fight for freedom.

When Sylvester came back from the war and was thrust back into the legalized segregation of the South, he found it very hard to adjust. He didn't think very much of the fact that we were still in the same condition, if not a little bit worse.

Rosa's brother, Sylvester McCauley, in uniform during World War II. (Courtesy of Rosa Parks)

A lot of black World War II veterans came back and tried to get registered to vote and could not. They found that they were treated with even more disrespect, especially if they were in uniform. Whites felt that things should remain as they had always been and that the black veterans were getting too sassy. My brother was one who could not take that kind of treatment anymore. Also, he could not find a job in Montgomery and did not want or expect anyone else to provide for him. He took his family and moved to Detroit, Michigan.

For some reason there were a lot of cases in 1949. I remember one especially. There were two youngsters from Newark, New Jersey, a sister and brother named Edwina Johnson, who was sixteen, and Marshall Johnson, who was fifteen. They came to Montgomery to visit, but no one told them about the segregation laws for the buses. They boarded a city bus and took seats in the white section. The driver, S. T. Lock, drew his pistol on them and kicked them off the bus. He must have called the police also, because the two teenagers were arrested and held in jail for two days. This was in July of 1949. Judge Wiley C. Hill threatened to send the children to reform school until they were twentyone years old, but I believe the NAACP managed to get them an attorney and they were just fined.

There were cases of violence against blacks all over, not just in Alabama. I remember a case in South Carolina. A black man named Isaac Woodard, Jr., was discharged from the Army in South Carolina and was on a bus and had his eyes put out by a white man who struck him across the head. The white man's name was Shore. The all-white jury was out just fifteen minutes before they acquitted Shore. Shore's attorney had stated to the jury, "If you rule against Shore, then let South Carolina secede again." He was referring to the fact that the southern states had seceded from the Union before the Civil War.

I remember 1949 as a very bad year. Things happened that most people never heard about, because they never were reported in the newspapers. At times I felt overwhelmed by all the violence and hatred, but there was nothing to do but keep going.

By that time I was both secretary of the Senior Branch of the NAACP, which was for the older people, and adviser to the NAACP Youth Council. I enjoyed working with young people. The high school students were the largest group in the Youth Council. One of our projects was getting the young people to try to take out books from the main library instead of going to the little branch across town that was the colored library.

The colored library did not have many books, and a student who wanted a book that wasn't there had to request it from the colored library, which in turn would order it from the main library. The student would have to return to the colored library to get the book. The members of the NAACP Youth Council went to the main library and asked for service there, saying that it was inconvenient for them to go to the colored library, which was quite far away. They did this again and again, but they were unsuccessful in changing the practice.

By the early 1950s Mr. E. D. Nixon had stepped

down as head of the Montgomery NAACP, but he was still very active in the organization. He was also president of the local branch of the Brotherhood of Sleeping Car Porters, so he used his union office downtown to conduct his community business. I did volunteer work for him at that office, just doing about the same thing as I had done at the NAACP office. He liked to say that I was the secretary for everything he had going. I answered telephones and letters and kept records on all the various cases of people who came to him for help. I was doing tailoring at Mr. Solon Crittenden's shop, and most evenings when I got off, I'd go by the office and do some work. I'd often take a sandwich to Mr. Nixon. When he wasn't working on the railroad, he was usually at the office.

It was Mr. Nixon who introduced me to Mrs. Virginia Durr. She was at his house, and he came by and picked me up to have me meet her. Mrs. Durr was a white woman, born and raised in Birmingham, who managed to overcome all the racism with which she grew up. She and her husband, Clifford, who was an attorney, did a lot for black people, and they didn't have many white friends as a result. I guess it was just the type of person she was, because her family believed in segregation.

I met her in 1954, and when she found out that I could sew, she hired me to do some work for her. I helped her with her daughter Lucy's wedding trousseau. I didn't make the wedding dress—I made the other garments. After that I sewed anything she needed done. She had an integrated prayer group that I was part of. African-American and Caucasian women would pray together mornings at her house. After a while that was broken up by the husbands and fathers and brothers of the white women. They took out ads in the papers repudiating their women.

I got to know Virginia quite well (at that time, when I was working for her, I called her Mrs. Durr even though she wanted me to call her by her first name). She told me that she had become conscious of racism when she had gone off to college in Massachusetts. One day she went into the college dining room, and there was a black girl at the table she was assigned to. Virginia had to make up her mind about whether she was going to sit next to the girl. She had never before sat down with a black person as an equal. So she chose to accept the fact that this young woman had the same right to sit there as the other students. She said she didn't ever regret that decision. Later she got married, and she and Mr. Durr were living in Washington, D.C., where he was a member of the Federal Communications Commission. When they talked about returning to Alabama, she had to decide if she wanted to, because she knew she and her husband didn't have the same attitude about segregation as most white people in Alabama did. In coming back to Alabama after being

An elementary classroom in Washington, D.C., one year after the
Brown v. Board of Education *ruling that school segregation
was unconstitutional. (U.S.N. & W.R. Collection,*
The Library of Congress)

away for twenty years, she wanted to be part of our
efforts to end segregation, even though that meant
being ostracized and made to suffer.

The year I met Mrs. Durr, 1954, the United States
Supreme Court handed down the famous decision
Brown v. *Board of Education* that declared segregated education unconstitutional. The NAACP had
been working for that for years and years, since
around 1925. They had attacked the issue of "separate but equal" education from all different angles,
because of course from whatever angle you looked
at it, education in the South was separate but not
equal. Just in my growing up, I had seen that.

97

Back in the 1920s and 1930s, the NAACP had started fighting for equal pay for black teachers. I remember that my mother used to talk about how black teachers were paid more poorly than white teachers. She finally left Montgomery County because the salaries for black teachers were so low. The NAACP helped black teachers in many parts of the South fight for equal salaries. They helped

Outside an integrated high school in Washington, D.C., after the U.S. Supreme Court declared segregated education unequal and unconstitutional. (U.S.N. & W.R. Collection, The Library of Congress)

the teachers in Birmingham, but it took a long time, something like seven years, from 1938 to 1945. You see, to file a suit on behalf of a lot of people—what they call a class action—you have to have a plaintiff, someone who will represent the others. It took a lot of courage to be a plaintiff. You could be risking your life. After the NAACP finally got the plaintiff in Birmingham, he was drafted into the Army, so there were a lot of delays. The NAACP and the teachers finally won, though, and pay equality started in the fall of 1945.

Before the NAACP brought suit in *Brown* v. *Board of Education* in 1951, about a dozen other suits against unequal elementary and high schools had been filed in Arkansas, Texas, North Carolina, Virginia, and Missouri by various organizations and groups, including the NAACP. But it was the *Brown* case in Topeka, Kansas, that finally went all the way to the U.S. Supreme Court for a decision. Two NAACP lawyers named Charles Hamilton Houston and Thurgood Marshall made it happen. Mr. Marshall even brought in a sociologist, Dr. Kenneth Clark, to testify that segregated education was bad for black children. Later, in the 1960s, Thurgood Marshall became the first black U.S. Supreme Court justice.

You can't imagine the rejoicing among black people, and some white people, when the Supreme Court decision came down in May 1954. The Court had said that separate education could not be equal, and many of us saw how the same idea applied to other things, like public transportation.

It was a very hopeful time. African Americans believed that at last there was a real chance to change the segregation laws. I remember that Fred Gray came back to Montgomery to open a law practice around that time. He was born and raised in Montgomery. When he was twelve, he became a minister in the Church of Christ. But his dedication to the ministry did not exempt him from the prejudice against people of color. Due to racial segregation, he had to go to the North to study and get his law degree. He could have stayed in the North and had an easier time, but he chose to come back to help in the fight for the rights of African Americans. I was really pleased when he opened up an office in downtown Montgomery and established a law practice. Now we had a second black attorney to advise us on legal matters.

Charles Langford was the other black attorney. Before Fred Gray opened his office, a black woman named Mahalia Ashley Dickerson, who had been a good friend of mine for years, had opened a law practice. But she had to leave Montgomery because she did not receive the support she needed from the African-American community. They did not give her enough business for her to make a living, and she was a single mother with triplet sons.

After the Supreme Court ruling in *Brown* v. *Board of Education,* we all waited to see what would happen next. The next question for the Supreme Court to decide was how to go about desegregating the schools. They didn't hear arguments about that until almost a year later, in April 1955. But in the meantime a lot of activist people were going ahead and making plans. Mrs. Durr told me about a workshop that was going to be held called "Racial Desegregation: Implementing the Supreme Court Decision." It was going to be at a place called the Highlander Folk School in Monteagle, Tennessee. She said that she thought I should go and that there was a scholarship available and she would get together the money to pay my expenses to go up there for this ten-day workshop. Mr. Nixon was all for my going too, and so I went. It was the summer of 1955.

Mrs. Durr wrote in her autobiography, *Outside the Magic Circle,* that I didn't have a suitcase or a bathing suit and that she gave me those things. I don't have quite the same recollection. She's right that I didn't have a suitcase, because I wasn't doing any traveling, but I didn't take one to Highlander either, as I recall. I did have a bathing suit, because in 1950 I went to Florida and I remember having one then. I was working for a family in Montgomery, doing their housework and looking after their little girl, who was about three years old and who had congenital asthma. They went on vacation to Florida, to a place called Sunnyside Beach on the Gulf of Mexico, and I went with them, and I had this little playsuit, because I went on the beach. They had a lake there at Highlander, but I never did get in that because I've never been much of a swimmer.

I don't remember what Parks had to say about my going to Highlander. I couldn't get him to go with me. He didn't like to travel away from home that much, but he didn't object to my going. My mother had come from Pine Level to live with us after World War II ended, and Parks and my mother could get along without me. He would cook. When he was quite young, his mother and grandmother were ill, and he had taken care of them.

I don't recall whether Mrs. Durr mentioned to me that Highlander was a white school. She didn't mention any race in particular. So I didn't really know what to expect when I got there. When I did get there, I found out that in the whole of Grundy County, Tennessee, there was not one black person other than those who came to the workshop and who stayed at Highlander. I didn't have any contact to speak of with the white people outside the school, but I knew they weren't at all happy about the school, because they had burned the building at the first opportunity they had.

I took a bus to Chattanooga, Tennessee, where a white man picked me up and drove me about fifty miles to Monteagle, Tennessee. I don't think we talked much, but I was not uncomfortable. I was used to white people, and I accepted them as they accepted me. The scenery was beautiful, and as we approached the school, I could see why it might have been called Highlander. It was on a plateau in the mountains that was surrounded by gardens and herds of cattle.

Myles Horton was the man who started the school back in 1932 during the Great Depression. He had the idea that people could solve their own problems with the right kind of guidance. When he opened the school, he concentrated on the problems of oppressed white workers in the Appalachian Mountains. He had workshops on labor relations, workers' rights, and race relations. By the 1950s he'd turned more to civil rights. The school offered workshops to train future leaders so they could go back home and work for change using what they had learned at the school. I think that was probably when the hostility from the white community started.

I met a black woman named Septima Clark at Highlander. She had lost her job as a teacher in Charleston, South Carolina. She had been an active member of the NAACP there and had made an attempt to get the black teachers paid an equal salary. She was also a friend of Judge William Waites Waring, who ruled against the Democratic Party being a private club so it would be open to everybody to

*Septima Clark and Rosa exchange ideas at the Highlander Folk
School, 1955. (Courtesy of Rosa Parks)*

vote in. At that time in South Carolina, blacks
couldn't register because the Democratic Party con-
sidered itself a private club. There was no Republi-
can Party to speak of in South Carolina at that time.

When I met her, Septima Poinsette Clark (she was
the daughter of a slave owned by the Poinsette family, after whom the poinsettia flower is named) was
in her late fifties and teaching citizenship classes at
Highlander. She was in charge of the "citizenship
school," and her job was to teach adults to read and
write and learn about basic citizenship so they could
become teachers of others, so they could register to

104

vote. She was very much at home at Highlander, but the outside community made it hard for her. They burned the building when Myles was away and she was there. They put her in jail and accused her of a lot of things, like drinking liquor and being a Communist. They didn't like the things she was doing. She later wrote a book about her life called *Echo in My Soul*, and she gave me a copy of it. And every Christmas she would send me a letter.

That summer I was there was the first year they had adult education. A black hairdresser named Bernice Robinson taught one class, which was held two nights a week and had fourteen students. She taught them basic things, like how to write their names, how to write a check, how to write a letter to someone in the Army. After that class ended, eight of the students passed the voting test.

I spent ten days at Highlander and went to different workshops, mostly on how to desegregate schools. Everything was very organized. We all had duties, and they were listed on a bulletin board each day. We shared the work and the play. One of my greatest pleasures there was enjoying the smell of bacon frying and coffee brewing and knowing that white folks were doing the preparing instead of me. There was swimming in the man-made lake, volleyball, square dancing. It was quite enjoyable to be with the people at Highlander. We forgot about what

Rosa (at right) confers with Dr. Fred Paterson (center), then president of the Tuskegee Institute, and Mr. James Johnson at the Highlander School. (Courtesy of Rosa Parks)

color anybody was. I was forty-two years old, and it was one of the few times in my life up to that point when I did not feel any hostility from white people. I experienced people of different races and backgrounds meeting together in workshops and living together in peace and harmony. I felt that I could express myself honestly without any repercussions or antagonistic attitudes from other people.

I could have stayed a while longer. It was hard to leave, knowing what I was going back to, but of course I knew I had to leave. So I went back to Montgomery and back to my job as an assistant tailor at Montgomery Fair department store, where you had to be smiling and polite no matter how rudely you were treated. And back to the city buses, with their segregation rules.

8

"You're Under Arrest"

I don't think any segregation law angered black people in Montgomery more than bus segregation. And that had been so since the laws about segregation on public transportation had been passed. That was back in 1900, and black people had boycotted Montgomery streetcars until the City Council changed its ordinance so that nobody would be forced to give up a seat unless there was another seat to move to. But over the years practices had changed, although the law had not. When I was put off the bus back in 1943, the bus driver was really acting against the law. In 1945, two years after that incident, the State of Alabama passed a law requiring that all bus companies under its jurisdiction enforce segregation. But that law did not spell out what bus drivers were supposed to do in a case like mine.

Here it was, half a century after the first segregation law, and there were 50,000 African Americans in Montgomery. More of us rode the buses than Caucasians did, because more whites could afford cars. It was very humiliating having to suffer the indignity of riding segregated buses twice a day, five days a week, to go downtown and work for white people.

There were incidents all the time. Mrs. Durr says that I would tell her about them time and time again. Mr. Nixon used to try to negotiate some small changes. I know Mr. Nixon said that at some point he went to the bus company about black people having to pay at the front door and then go around to the back door to enter. They told him, "Your folks started it. They do it because they want to."

Another time he went to see about extending the route of the Day Street bus. Black people in a little community on the other side of the Day Street Bridge had to walk across the bridge, about half a mile, to get to the bus. Mr. Nixon went down to the bus company to protest. He was always going down to the bus company to protest; sometimes he went by himself, sometimes he took someone with him. He himself did not ride the buses—he had his own car; but he was acting on behalf of the community. The bus company told him that as long as the people were willing to walk the half mile and then pay to ride the rest of the way downtown, they had no need to extend the bus line.

Jo Ann Robinson was an English professor at Alabama State College. Back in 1946 she had helped found the Women's Political Council. Over the years she'd had her share of run-ins with bus drivers, but at first she couldn't get the other women in the Council to get indignant. She was from Cleveland, Ohio, and most of them were natives of Montgomery. When she complained about the rudeness of the bus drivers, they said that was a fact of life in Montgomery. She had often brought protests to the bus company on behalf of the Women's Political Council. Finally she managed to get the company to agree that the buses would stop at every corner in black neighborhoods, just as they did in the white neighborhoods. But this was a very small victory.

What galled her, and many more of us, was that blacks were over sixty-six percent of the riders. It was unfair to segregate us. But neither the bus company nor the mayor nor the city commissioners would listen. I remember having discussions about how a boycott of the city buses would really hurt the bus company in its pocketbook. But I also remember asking a few people if they would be willing to stay off the buses to make things better for us, and them saying that they had too far to go to work. So it didn't seem as if there would be much support for a boycott. The Montgomery NAACP was beginning to think about filing suit against the city of Montgomery over bus segregation. But they had to have the right plaintiff and a strong case. The best plaintiff would be a woman, because a woman would get more sympathy than a man. And the woman would have to be above reproach, have a good reputation, and have done nothing wrong but refuse to give up her seat.

Back in the spring of 1955 a teenage girl named Claudette Colvin and an elderly woman refused to give up their seats in the middle section of a bus to white people. When the driver went to get the police, the elderly woman got off the bus, but Claudette refused to leave, saying she had already paid her dime and had no reason to move. When the police came, they dragged her from the bus and arrested her. Now, her name was familiar to me, and it turned out that Claudette Colvin was the great-granddaughter of Mr. Gus Vaughn, the unmixed black man with all the children back in Pine Level who refused to work for the white man. His great-granddaughter must have inherited his sense of pride. I took a particular interest in the girl and her case.

After Claudette's arrest, a group of activists took a petition to the bus company officials and city officials. The petition asked for more courteous treatment and for no visible signs of segregation. They didn't ask for the end of the segregation, just for an understanding that whites would start sitting at the front of the bus and blacks would start sitting at the back, and wherever they met would be the dividing line. I think that petition also asked that black bus drivers be hired. The city officials and the bus company took months to answer that petition, and when they did, every request in it was turned down.

I did not go down with the others to present that petition to the bus company and the city officials, because I didn't feel anything could be accomplished. I had decided that I would not go anywhere with a piece of paper in my hand asking white folks for any favors. I had made that decision myself, as an individual.

I did meet with Claudette, along with Mr. Nixon and Jo Ann Robinson, and talked about taking her case to the federal courts. Claudette was willing, and we started making plans to raise money for her defense by having her speak in various parts of town. Everything was going along fine until Mr. Nixon discovered that Claudette was pregnant. She wasn't married, and so that was the end of that case. If the white press got hold of that information, they would have a field day. They'd call her a bad girl, and her case wouldn't have a chance. So the decision was made to wait until we had a plaintiff who was more upstanding before we went ahead and invested any more time and effort and money.

Another bus incident involving a woman occurred that summer. I didn't know much about the girl. Her name was Louise Smith, and she was about eighteen years old. They say she paid her fine and didn't protest. Hers certainly wasn't a good case for Mr. Nixon to appeal to a higher court.

I knew they needed a plaintiff who was beyond

reproach, because I was in on the discussions about the possible court cases. But that is not why I refused to give up my bus seat to a white man on Thursday, December 1, 1955. I did not intend to get arrested. If I had been paying attention, I wouldn't even have gotten on that bus.

I was very busy at that particular time. I was getting an NAACP workshop together for the 3rd and 4th of December, and I was trying to get the consent of Mr. H. Council Trenholm at Alabama State to have the Saturday meeting at the college. He did give permission, but I had a hard time getting to him to get permission to use the building. I was also getting the notices in the mail for the election of officers of the Senior Branch of the NAACP, which would be the next week.

When I got off from work that evening of December 1, I went to Court Square as usual to catch the Cleveland Avenue bus home. I didn't look to see who was driving when I got on, and by the time I recognized him, I had already paid my fare. It was the same driver who had put me off the bus back in 1943, twelve years earlier. He was still tall and heavy, with red, rough-looking skin. And he was still mean-looking. I didn't know if he had been on that route before—they switched the drivers around sometimes. I do know that most of the time if I saw him on a bus, I wouldn't get on it.

I saw a vacant seat in the middle section of the

The "colored" section at the back of the bus. (Courtesy of NAACP Public Relations)

bus and took it. I didn't even question why there was a vacant seat even though there were quite a few people standing in the back. If I had thought about it at all, I would probably have figured maybe someone saw me get on and did not take the seat but left it vacant for me. There was a man sitting next to the window and two women across the aisle.

The next stop was the Empire Theater, and some whites got on. They filled up the white seats, and one man was left standing. The driver looked back and noticed the man standing. Then he looked back at us. He said, "Let me have those front seats," because they were the front seats of the black section. Didn't anybody move. We just sat right where we were, the four of us. Then he spoke a second time: "Y'all better make it light on yourselves and let me have those seats."

The man in the window seat next to me stood up, and I moved to let him pass by me, and then I looked across the aisle and saw that the two women were also standing. I moved over to the window seat. I could not see how standing up was going to "make it light" for me. The more we gave in and complied, the worse they treated us.

I thought back to the time when I used to sit up all night and didn't sleep, and my grandfather would have his gun right by the fireplace, or if he had his one-horse wagon going anywhere, he always had his gun in the back of the wagon. People always say that I didn't give up my seat because I was tired, but that isn't true. I was not tired physically, or no more tired than I usually was at the end of a working day. I was not old, although some people have an image of me as being old then. I was forty-two. No, the only tired I was, was tired of giving in.

The driver of the bus saw me still sitting there, and he asked was I going to stand up. I said, "No." He said, "Well, I'm going to have you arrested." Then I said, "You may do that." These were the only words we said to each other. I didn't even know his name, which was James Blake, until we were in court together. He got out of the bus and stayed outside for a few minutes, waiting for the police.

As I sat there, I tried not to think about what might happen. I knew that anything was possible. I could be manhandled or beaten. I could be arrested. People have asked me if it occurred to me then that I could be the test case the NAACP had been looking for. I did not think about that at all. In fact if I had let myself think too deeply about what might happen to me, I might have gotten off the bus. But I chose to remain.

Meanwhile there were people getting off the bus and asking for transfers, so that began to loosen up the crowd, especially in the back of the bus. Not everyone got off, but everybody was very quiet. What conversation there was, was in low tones; no one was talking out loud. It would have been quite interesting to have seen the whole bus empty out. Or if the other three had stayed where they were, because if they'd had to arrest four of us instead of one, then that would have given me a little support. But it didn't matter. I never thought hard of them at all and never even bothered to criticize them.

Eventually two policemen came. They got on the bus, and one of them asked me why I didn't stand up. I asked him, "Why do you all push us around?" He said to me, and I quote him exactly, "I don't know, but the law is the law and you're under arrest." One policeman picked up my purse, and the second one picked up my shopping bag and escorted me to the squad car. In the squad car they returned my personal belongings to me. They did not put their hands on me or force me into the car. After I was seated in the car, they went back to the driver and asked him if he wanted to swear out a warrant. He answered that he would finish his route and then come straight back to swear out the warrant. I was only in custody, not legally arrested, until the warrant was signed.

As they were driving me to the city desk, at City Hall, near Court Street, one of them asked me again, "Why didn't you stand up when the driver spoke to you?" I did not answer. I remained silent all the way to City Hall.

As we entered the building, I asked if I could have a drink of water, because my throat was real dry. There was a fountain, and I was standing right next to it. One of the policemen said yes, but by the time I bent down to drink, another policeman said, "No, you can't drink no water. You have to wait until you get to the jail." So I was denied the chance to drink a sip of water. I was not going to do anything but wet my throat. I wasn't going to drink a whole lot of water, even though I was quite thirsty. That made me angry, but I did not respond.

At the city desk they filled out the necessary forms as I answered questions such as what my name was and where I lived. I asked if I could make a telephone call and they said, "No." Since that was my first arrest, I didn't know if that was more discrimination because I was black or if it was standard practice. But it seemed to me to be more discrimination. Then they escorted me back to the squad car, and we went to the city jail on North Ripley Street.

I wasn't frightened at the jail. I was more resigned than anything else. I don't recall being real angry, not enough to have an argument. I was just prepared to accept whatever I had to face. I asked again if I could make a telephone call. I was ignored.

They told me to put my purse on the counter and to empty my pockets of personal items. The only thing I had in my pocket was a tissue. I took that out. They didn't search me or handcuff me.

I was then taken to an area where I was finger-printed and where mug shots were taken. A white matron came to escort me to my jail cell, and I asked again if I might use the telephone. She told me that she would find out.

She took me up a flight of stairs (the cells were on the second level), through a door covered with iron mesh, and along a dimly lighted corridor. She placed me in an empty dark cell and slammed the door closed. She walked a few steps away, but then she turned around and came back. She said, "There are two girls around the other side, and if you want to go over there with them instead of being in a cell by yourself, I will take you over there." I told her that it didn't matter, but she said, "Let's go around there, and then you won't have to be in a cell alone." It was her way of being nice. It didn't make me feel any better.

As we walked to the other cell, I asked her again, "May I use the telephone?" She answered that she would check.

There were two black women in the cell that the matron took me to, as she had said. One of them spoke to me and the other didn't. One just acted as if I wasn't there. The one who spoke to me asked me what had happened to me. I told her that I was arrested on the bus.

She said, "Some of those bus drivers sure are mean. You married?"

I said, "Yes," and she said, "Your husband ain't going to let you stay in here."

She wanted to know if there was anything she could do, and I said, "If you have a cup, I could drink a little water." She had a dark metal mug hanging above the toilet, and she caught a little water from the tap, and I took two swallows of that. She then started telling me about her problems. I became interested in her story and wondered how I could assist her.

She said she had been there for fifty-five or fifty-seven days and that she was a widow, her husband had died. She'd been keeping company with another man, and he'd got angry with her and struck her. She took a hatchet and went after him, and he had her arrested.

She said she had two brothers, but she had not been able to get in touch with them. Meanwhile, after she'd been in jail for a certain length of time, the man had kind of healed up and he wanted to get her out of jail, but only providing that she would keep on going with him. But she didn't want any more to do with him. So she was in jail without any way of getting in touch with anybody who could get her out.

She had a pencil but no paper, and I didn't have any either, because they had taken my purse. By the time she got through telling me about what was going on, the matron returned and told me to come out of the cell. I did not know where I was going until we reached the telephone booth. She gave me a card and told me to write down who I was calling and the telephone number. She placed a dime in the slot, dialed the number, and stayed close by to hear what I was saying.

I called home. My husband and mother were both there. She answered the telephone. I said, "I'm in jail. See if Parks will come down here and get me out."

She wanted to know, "Did they beat you?"

I said, "No, I wasn't beaten, but I am in jail."

She handed him the telephone, and I said, "Parks, will you come get me out of jail?"

He said, "I'll be there in a few minutes." He didn't have a car, so I knew it would be longer. But while we were still on the phone, a friend came by in his car. He'd heard about my being in jail and had driven to our place on Cleveland Court to see if he could help. He said he'd drive Parks to the jail.

The matron then took me back to the cell.

As Parks' friend had indicated, the word was already out about my arrest. Mr. Nixon had been notified by his wife, who was told by a neighbor, Bertha Butler, who had seen me escorted off the bus.

Mr. Nixon called the jail to find out what the charge was, but they wouldn't tell him. Then he had tried to reach Fred Gray, one of the two black lawyers in Montgomery, but he wasn't home. So finally Mr. Nixon called Clifford Durr, the white lawyer who was Mrs. Virginia Durr's husband. Mr. Durr called the jail and found out that I'd been arrested under the segregation laws. He also found out what the bail was.

Meanwhile Parks had called a white man he knew who could raise the bail. His friend took him over to the man's house to pick him up. I don't remember how much the bail was.

When I got back to the cell, the woman had found some little crumpled-up paper, and she wrote both of her brothers' names and telephone numbers on it. She said to call them early in the morning because they went to work around six A.M. I told her I would.

Just then the matron came to let me know that I was being released, and the woman hadn't given me the piece of paper. They were rushing me out, and she was right behind me. She knew she would not get through the iron-mesh door at the end of the stairs, so she threw it down the stairs and it landed right in front of me. I picked it up and put it in my pocket.

Mrs. Durr was the first person I saw as I came through the iron mesh door with matrons on either side of me. There were tears in her eyes, and she seemed shaken, probably wondering what they had done to me. As soon as they released me, she put her arms around me, and hugged and kissed me as if we were sisters.

I was real glad to see Mr. Nixon and Attorney Durr too. We went to the desk, where I picked up my personal belongings and was given a trial date. Mr. Nixon asked that the date be the following Monday, December 5, 1955, explaining that he was a Pullman porter and would be out of Montgomery until then. We left without very much conversation, but it was an emotional moment. I didn't realize how much being in jail had upset me until I got out.

As we were going down the stairs, Parks and his friends were driving up, so I got in the car with them, and Mr. Nixon followed us home.

By the time I got home, it was about nine-thirty or ten at night. My mother was glad to have me home and wanted to know what she could do to make me comfortable. I told her I was hungry (for some reason I had missed lunch that day), and she prepared some food for me. Mrs. Durr and my friend Bertha Butler were there, and they helped my mother. I was thinking about having to go to work the next day, but I knew I would not get to bed anytime soon.

Everyone was angry about what had happened to

me and talking about how it should never happen again. I knew that I would never, never ride another segregated bus, even if I had to walk to work. But it still had not occurred to me that mine could be a test case against the segregated buses.

Then Mr. Nixon asked if I would be willing to make my case a test case against segregation. I told him I'd have to talk with my mother and husband. Parks was pretty angry. He thought it would be as difficult to get people to support me as a test case as it had been to develop a test case out of Claudette Colvin's experience. We discussed and debated the question for a while. In the end Parks and my mother supported the idea. They were against segregation and were willing to fight it. And I had worked on enough cases to know that a ruling could not be made without a plaintiff. So I agreed to be the plaintiff.

9

"They've Messed With the Wrong One Now"

Mr. Nixon was happy as could be when I told him yes. I don't recall exactly what he said, but according to him, he said, "My God, look what segregation has put in my hands." What he meant by that was that I was a perfect plaintiff. "Rosa Parks worked with me for twelve years prior to this," he would tell reporters later. "She was secretary for everything I had going—the Brotherhood of Sleeping Car Porters, NAACP, Alabama Voters' League, all of those things. I knew she'd stand on her feet. She was honest, she was clean, she had integrity. The press couldn't go out and dig up something she did last year, or last month, or five years ago. They couldn't hang nothing like that on Rosa Parks."

I had no police record, I'd worked all my life, I wasn't pregnant with an illegitimate child. The white people couldn't point to me and say that there was anything I had done to deserve such treatment except to be born black.

Meanwhile Fred Gray, the black attorney, had called Jo Ann Robinson and told her about my arrest. She got in touch with other leaders of the Women's Political Council, and they agreed to call for a boycott of the buses starting Monday, December 5, the day of my trial. So on the Thursday night I was arrested, they met at midnight at Alabama State, cut a mimeograph stencil, and ran off 35,000 handbills. The next morning she and some of her students loaded the handbills into her car, and she drove to all the local black elementary and junior high and high schools to drop them off so the students could take them home to their parents.

This is what the handbill said:

This is for Monday, December 5, 1955.

Another Negro woman has been arrested and thrown into jail because she refused to get up out of her seat on the bus and give it to a white person.

It is the second time since the Claudette Colvin case that a Negro woman has been arrested for the same thing. This has to be stopped.

Negroes have rights, too, for if Negroes did not ride the buses, they could not operate. Three-fourths of the riders are Negroes, yet we are arrested, or have to stand over empty seats. If we do not do something to stop these arrests, they will continue. The next time it may be you, or your daughter, or mother.

This woman's case will come up on Monday. We are, therefore, asking every Negro to stay off the buses

Monday in protest of the arrest and trial. Don't ride the buses to work, to town, to school, or anywhere on Monday.

You can afford to stay out of school for one day. If you work, take a cab, or walk. But please, children and grown-ups, don't ride the bus at all on Monday. Please stay off all buses Monday.

Early that Friday morning, Mr. Nixon called the Reverend Ralph David Abernathy, minister of the First Baptist Church. Mr. Nixon had decided that black ministers could do more to mobilize support in the community than anyone else. He also called eighteen other ministers and arranged a meeting for that evening. Mr. Nixon had to work as a porter on the Montgomery–Atlanta–New York route, so he would be unable to attend, but he talked to them all about what he wanted them to do.

Then he called a white reporter for the *Montgomery Advertiser* named Joe Azbell and arranged a meeting down at Union Station to show him one of the handbills. Mr. Nixon wanted the story on the front page. Joe Azbell said he would see what he could do. Meanwhile, the story of my arrest was reported in a small article in that day's paper.

The first thing I did the morning after I went to jail was to call the number the woman in the cell with me had written down on that crumpled piece of paper. I reached one of her brothers and let him know why I was calling. He just said, "Okay," or something like that. We didn't have any more conversation. I just told him that his sister said she would like him to come and see her.

I saw her about two days later. I was on my way up Dorsey Street to go to one of those meetings—after the boycott got started, people met all the time, anytime they thought they could call somebody together. I didn't recognize her. She was dressed up and looked real nice. She was clean and had her hair fixed nicely. I was going along and she said, "Hi. How are you?" Then she said, "You don't know me?" I said, "No." She said, "I was the one who was in jail with you." I said, "I am glad to see you out." I didn't think to ask her for her name or address or telephone number, and I just hurried on. That was the only time I've ever seen her. She sure did look good.

On the morning of Friday, December 2, after I made that call I promised to make, I called Felix Thomas, who operated a cab company, and took a cab to work. I was not going to ride the bus anymore. Mr. John Ball, who was in charge of men's alterations at Montgomery Fair, was surprised to see me. He said, "I didn't think you would be here. I thought you would be a nervous wreck." I said, "Why should going to jail make a nervous wreck out of me?" And then as soon as I got off for lunch, I went to Fred Gray's office.

Ever since Fred had opened his law practice in Montgomery, I had often done that. I'd pick up something from the store for my lunch. He usually brought his lunch. We would eat lunch together, and then sometimes I would answer the telephone while he ran out and did an errand or something, and then it was time for me to go back to work. Fred didn't have a secretary, and I often helped him out. The day after I was arrested, Fred Gray's office was like a beehive. People were calling and dropping by to ask about the boycott and the meeting the ministers had called for that night.

After work, I went to that meeting at the Dexter Avenue Baptist Church. I explained how I had been arrested, and then there were long discussions about what to do. Some of the ministers wanted to talk about how to support the protest, but others wanted to talk about whether or not to have a protest. Many of them left the meeting before any decisions were made. But most of those who stayed agreed to talk about the protest in their Sunday sermons and to hold another meeting on Monday evening to decide if the protest should continue. A group of ministers at that meeting formed a committee to draft a shorter leaflet that was basically a condensation of the leaflet that Jo Ann Robinson and the others of the

Women's Political Council had written. It said:

> Don't ride the bus to work, to town, to school, or any
> place on Monday, December 5.
>
> Another Negro woman has been arrested and put in jail
> because she refused to give up her bus seat.
>
> Don't ride the buses to work, to town, to school, or
> anywhere on Monday. If you work, take a cab, or share
> a ride, or walk.
>
> Come to a mass meeting, Monday at 7:00 P.M., at the
> Holt Street Baptist Church for further instruction.

On Sunday the *Montgomery Advertiser* ran a copy
of Jo Ann Robinson's handbill on the front page, and
that helped spread the word to people who might
have missed the leaflets or didn't go to church. But
no one could be sure if the protest would be successful. Just because they read a leaflet or heard about
it in church, it didn't mean that people would stay
away from the buses. All eighteen black-owned cab
companies in Montgomery had agreed to make stops
at all the bus stops and charge only ten cents, the
same fare as on the buses. But people would have
to wait for a cab that had room for them. To make
matters worse, it looked like rain for Monday.

The sky was dark on Monday morning, but that
didn't make any difference. Most black people had
finally had enough of segregation on the buses. They
stayed off those buses. They waited at the bus stops

With no black business the buses often had few or no riders. (Photo by Dan Weiner, courtesy of Sandra Weiner)

for the black-owned cabs to come along. Or they walked or got a ride. As a result, the Montgomery city buses were practically empty. Oh, a few black people took the buses, but they were mostly people who had not heard about the protest. Some of them were scared away from the buses. The city police had vowed to protect anyone who wanted to ride, and each bus had two motorcycle escorts. But some of the people who didn't know what was going on thought the police were there to arrest them for riding the buses, not to protect them. And then there were those few who didn't want to be inconvenienced. When the bus they were on passed a bus stop full of black people waiting for cabs, they ducked down low so nobody would see them.

That day I had no idea what the result was going to be, but I think everybody was quite amazed at that demonstration of people staying off the buses. It was a surprise to everybody, I think. As Mr. Nixon said, "We surprised ourselves." Never before had black people demonstrated so clearly how much those city buses depended on their business. More important, never before had the black community of Montgomery united in protest against segregation on the buses.

I didn't go to work that Monday. Instead that morning I went down to the courthouse for my trial. Parks went with me. I did not spend a lot of time planning what to wear, but I remember very clearly that I wore a straight, long-sleeved black dress with a white collar and cuffs, a small black velvet hat with pearls across the top, and a charcoal-gray coat. I carried a black purse and wore white gloves. I was not especially nervous. I knew what I had to do.

A lot of folks were down at the courthouse. Some people couldn't get in. Parks was almost prohibited from entering the courthouse. But when he said he was my husband, he was permitted to enter. You could hardly see the street for the crowds. Many members of the NAACP Youth Council were there, and they were all shouting their support.

There was a girl in the crowd named Mary Frances. She had a high-pitched voice, and it just came through the air: "Oh, she's so sweet. They've messed with the wrong one now." She said it like a little chant, "They've messed with the wrong one now."

It wasn't a long trial. The bus driver was the main prosecution witness. Only then did I learn what his name was. Since that time I have read a little more about him. He was born James P. Blake in Seman, Alabama, in Elmore County. Seman is a few miles south of Equality, Alabama, which was a pretty strange name for a town in such a segregated state. He was nine and a half months older than I was. He left school after the ninth grade. His wife was named Edna, and they moved to Montgomery in 1939. He got his job as a bus driver with the Montgomery City Lines in 1942. He was drafted into the army the following year and served in Europe. In 1945 he returned to Montgomery and his job as a bus driver. He stayed on that job until 1972, when he retired.

The prosecution also called as a witness a white woman who testified that there had been a vacant seat in the back of the bus and that I had refused to take it. This was not true. Later I learned that Professor J. E. Pierce, who had served with me on the NAACP defense committee for Andy Wright, was very upset about the woman's statement. He told Mr. Nixon, "You can always find some damn white woman to lie."

I was not called to testify in my own behalf. Although my lawyers, Charles Langford and Fred Gray, entered a plea of "Not Guilty" for me, they did not intend to try to defend me against the charges. The point of making mine a test case was to allow me to be found guilty and then to appeal the conviction to a higher court. Only in higher courts could the segregation laws actually be changed, because the judges in the local courts were not going to do anything to change the way things were. So I was found guilty of violating the segregation laws and given a suspended sentence. I was fined $10.00, plus $4.00 in court costs. The crowd reacted angrily, but there was no organized protest.

I didn't go home after my trial was over. Instead I stayed downtown. I wanted to know what I could do. Fred Gray said he would appreciate it if I would stay in his office and answer the telephone, so I did. As soon as I got there, the telephone started ringing, because people had heard the news. I never did tell anybody who called that I was the one they were calling about. I just answered the phone and took messages. When Fred came back, Mr. Nixon took me home. It was getting pretty close to night, and I had to go home to get ready for the meeting at the Holt Street Baptist Church that evening.

Earlier that day Reverend Abernathy, who was about twenty-nine years old at the time, and some other ministers had met and decided to form the Montgomery Improvement Association (MIA). Mr. Nixon was there, and so was Fred Gray. The reason they wanted to form a brand-new organization was that they thought it would be better than just leaving the organizing to an established group like the NAACP. The NAACP was a relatively weak organization in Alabama; it was not a mass organization. Membership was kind of small, and you could hardly get people to join. They also wanted to rule out the NAACP so that the powers that be could not charge that this demonstration, this show of strength, was being led by outside agitators. That's what the whites liked to do, say that any trouble was caused by outside agitators. They refused to believe that black people in Montgomery had the courage to stand up for their rights.

So they met that afternoon, and then they decided they should elect a president, and they elected the Reverend Martin Luther King, Jr., pastor of the Dexter Avenue Baptist Church.

At the time I didn't know Dr. King. I had met him in August 1955 when he was guest speaker at an NAACP meeting, but I didn't often attend the Dexter Avenue Baptist Church, which was right across the street from the big white state capitol building with its Confederate flag. I found out later that I knew his wife, Coretta. I did not know her well, but I had been to concerts where she sang. I didn't even know she was married to a minister.

Dr. King was new to Montgomery, and Dr. Abernathy had been trying to get him active in civil-rights work. Rufus Lewis attended Dexter Avenue Baptist Church and had a very good opinion of Dr. King. Rufus Lewis had an exclusive nightclub—only registered voters could go there. It was Rufus Lewis who nominated Dr. King to be president of the MIA.

The advantage of having Dr. King as president was that he was so new to Montgomery and to civil-rights work that he hadn't been there long enough to make any strong friends or enemies. Mr. Nixon thought he was a good choice. As he told the people who wrote *Eyes on the Prize: America's Civil Rights Years 1954–1965:*

> Rev. King was a young man, a very intelligent young man. He had not been there long enough for the city fathers to put their hand on him. Usually they'd find some young man just come to town . . . pat him on the shoulder and tell him what a nice church he got. [They'd say], "Reverend, your suit don't look so nice to represent the so-and-so Baptist Church" . . . and they'd get him a suit. . . . You'd have to watch out for that kind of thing. *(Page 73)*

That's why so many influential blacks in the South were so conservative: They had accepted favors from the white people and didn't want to offend them. We found that over and over in our voter-registration drives. Some of the biggest names in the African-American community were not registered to vote. There was a man named R. R. Pierce from Lowndes County who was the principal of the school there. Nobody ever did get him to try to register.

That night they had the meeting at the Holt Street Baptist Church, which was right in the black community so people wouldn't be afraid to attend. They didn't know how many people to expect, and they were not prepared for how many showed up. People filled that church, and hundreds more stood outside, so they set up a loudspeaker system so those people outside could hear what was going on inside. The meeting was already on when I got there, and I had a hard time getting into the church because there were so many people, inside and outside. I made it to the platform, and they gave me a seat.

The main thing they wanted to decide at that meeting was whether to continue the boycott. Some people thought we should quit while we were still ahead. And hardly anybody thought the boycott could go longer than the end of the week, which was four more days. If it did, it could be very dangerous, because everyone knew the whites wouldn't stand for it.

Mr. Nixon spoke first, as I recall. He was probably worried that people wouldn't really support a long boycott. He remembered all those years when it had been impossible to get black people to stand together. He said, "You who are afraid, you better get your hat and coat and go home. This is going to be a long-drawn-out affair. I want to tell you something: For years and years I've been talking about how I didn't want the children who came along behind me to have to suffer the indignities that I've suffered all these years. Well, I've changed my mind—I want to enjoy some of that freedom myself."

Dr. King was introduced to the audience as the president of the new Montgomery Improvement Association. He was a fine speaker, and he gave a speech that really got the crowd excited. This is part of what he said:

> There comes a time that people get tired. We are here this evening to say to those who have mistreated us so long that we are tired—tired of being segregated and humiliated; tired of being kicked about by the brutal feet of oppression. . . . For many years we have shown amazing patience. We have sometimes given our white brothers the feeling that we like the way we are being treated. But we come here tonight to be saved from that patience that makes us patient with anything less than freedom and justice. One of the great glories of democracy is the right to protest for right. . . . [I]f you will protest courageously and yet with dignity and Christian love, when the history books are written in future

The Reverend Martin Luther King, Jr., speaks at a mass meeting of bus boycotters. (Photo by Dan Weiner, courtesy of Sandra Weiner)

generations the historians will pause and say, "There lived a great people—a black people—who injected new meaning and dignity into the veins of civilization." That is our challenge and our overwhelming responsibility. *(Eyes on the Prize, page 76)*

He received loud cheers and applause and *Amen*s. Then I was introduced. I had asked did they want me to say anything. They said, "You have had enough and you have said enough and you don't have to speak." So I didn't speak. The other people spoke. I didn't feel any particular need to speak. I enjoyed listening to the others and seeing the enthusiasm of the audience.

After that the Reverend Ralph Abernathy read the list of demands that the Montgomery Improvement Association was going to present to the bus company and the city's white leaders. There were three demands: 1) Courteous treatment on the buses; 2) First-come, first-served seating, with whites in front and blacks in back; 3) Hiring of black drivers for the black bus routes. Then he asked the audience to vote on these demands by standing if they wanted to continue the boycott and make the demands. People started getting up, one or two at a time at first, and then more and more, until every single person in that church was standing, and outside the crowd was cheering "Yes!"

10

Stride Toward Freedom

The following Thursday, December 8, Dr. King and Attorney Fred Gray and others met with the three Montgomery city commissioners and representatives of the bus company. They presented the three demands. The bus company people denied that the drivers were discourteous to black riders and would not hear of hiring any black drivers on the predominantly black routes. They also said the first-come, first-served seating arrangement was in violation of the city's segregation laws. Fred Gray said that wasn't true and that the same bus company allowed that type of arrangement in the city of Mobile, Alabama. But they wouldn't change their minds.

The city commissioners wouldn't go along with any of the demands either. They didn't want to give an inch, not even to reasonable demands. They were afraid of compromising in any way with black people.

The boycott lasted through that week, and then through the next. No one had any idea how long it would last. Some people said it couldn't last, but it seemed like those who said that were the white people and not us. The whites did everything they could do to stop it.

The police started getting after the groups of blacks who were waiting at the bus stops for the black-owned cabs to pick them up. Then they threatened to arrest the cab drivers if they did not charge their regular fare, which I think was forty-five cents, to go downtown instead of ten cents like the buses charged. White private citizens resisted the boycott too.

A lot of people lost their jobs because they supported the boycott. Both Parks and I lost our jobs, but neither of us was fired. He resigned. Mr. Armstrong, the white owner of the private barbering concession at Maxwell Field Air Force base, issued an order that there was to be no discussion of "the bus protest or Rosa Parks in his establishment." Parks said he would not work anywhere where his wife's name could not be mentioned.

I was discharged from Montgomery Fair department store in January of 1956, but I was not told by the personnel officer that it was because of the boycott. I do not like to form in my mind an idea that I don't have any proof of. The young man who ran the tailor shop at Montgomery Fair had opened his own shop down the street, and he stayed at the store through Christmas only because he wanted to get his bonus money. Then the first week of January he was just going to work full-time in his own shop. So the explanation they gave me about not keeping me on was that they didn't have a tailor. Of course, I could do the stitching work, the work of the shop, but I had never been required to do any fitting of men's clothing in the store. The young man who was working as a helper didn't have any experience in fitting at all. They closed the shop. They gave me two weeks' pay and my bonus money, and I went home.

This was a blessing in a way, I guess, because then I didn't have to worry about how I was going to get to and from work without riding the buses. After that I worked at home, taking in sewing. I started traveling quite a bit, making appearances because of my arrest and the boycott. And then I did work for the MIA.

I was on the executive board of directors of the MIA and I did whatever was needed. I dispensed clothing and shoes to people who needed them. We had an abundance of clothing and shoes sent to us from all parts of the country. Many people needed those things because they were out of work and unable to buy clothing. Those who had jobs wore out many pairs of shoes walking to and from work. I also worked for a short while as a dispatcher for the MIA Transportation Committee.

When the police started arresting cab drivers for

During the boycott, blacks relied on a sophisticated system of volunteer cabs. The E.L. Posey parking lot was one of the most important stops. (Photo by Dan Weiner, courtesy of Sandra Weiner)

not charging full fare, the MIA asked for volunteer drivers. Jo Ann Robinson was one. The churches collected money and bought several station wagons. Ordinary black people contributed, and so did some important white people in Montgomery, like the Durrs. As a dispatcher, I was responsible for taking calls from people who needed rides and then

144

making calls to the drivers of private cars and the church station wagons to see that the people were picked up wherever they were.

After a while quite a sophisticated system was developed. There were twenty private cars and fourteen station wagons. There were thirty-two pickup and transfer sites, and scheduled service from five-thirty in the morning until twelve-thirty at night. About 30,000 people were transported to and from work every day.

What about the other people who usually rode the buses? Well, I don't have numbers, but a lot of them were transported by their employers. Some of the white women couldn't get along without their maids. A lot of white women drove their housekeepers and cooks to and from work every day. The mayor appealed to them not to help the boycott in this way. He said that the boycott was successful because the white women were taking all the maids back and forth. But the white women wouldn't stop. They said, "Well, if the mayor wants to come and do my washing and ironing and look after my children and clean my house and cook my meals, he can do it. But I'm not getting rid of my maid."

The police tried to stop all this. They would arrest the black car-pool drivers for every minor traffic violation. And there were threatening telephone calls and anonymous letters to the white people. One typical letter read:

Dear Friend:
   Listed below are a few of the white people who are
still hauling their Negro maids. This must be stopped.
These people would appreciate a call from you, day or
night. Let's let them know how we feel about them
hauling Negroes.

The Montgomery Improvement Association held
regular meetings, every Monday and Thursday night,
to keep the people inspired and to talk about the
latest problems and what to do about them. January
came. The white people were getting angrier and
angrier. I remember somebody said that the mem-
berships of the Montgomery chapters of the Ku Klux
Klan and the White Citizens' Council went way up
during that time. Even Mayor W. A. Gayle went out
and joined the White Citizens' Council and was
proud to announce it in public.

   Late in January the three city commissioners met
with three black ministers who were not part of
the MIA. These ministers agreed to a plan for bus
seating that would reserve ten seats in front for
whites and ten seats in back for blacks, with the
rest available first-come, first-served. Then the
commission told the *Montgomery Advertiser*, and
that Sunday the paper ran big headlines announcing
the end of the boycott. But Dr. King and the Reverend Abernathy and the other leaders of the MIA
heard what was happening. They went all over the
black community Saturday night saying it was a lie.

Then on Sunday the ministers told their congregations the story wasn't true. So they got the word out and very few black people rode the buses on Monday.

Now Mayor Gayle announced that he would no longer negotiate with the boycotters, although we didn't see that he'd been doing much negotiating anyhow. He called the leaders of the boycott a bunch of Negro radicals. There was real violence against the people by this time. Dr. King's home was bombed at the end of January. Two days later Mr. Nixon's home was bombed. Nobody tried to bomb my home, but I did get a lot of threatening telephone calls. They'd say things like, "You're the cause of all this. You should be killed." It was frightening to get those calls, and it really bothered me when Mama answered the telephone and it was one of those calls.

In early February Fred Gray filed suit in U.S. District Court saying that bus segregation was unconstitutional. By that time the appeal of my case had been thrown out on a technicality, meaning my conviction was upheld. The new suit was our way of getting tough. The City Commission and the bus company and the mayor wouldn't even agree that bus drivers were not polite. Fred Gray wanted to challenge the whole bus-segregation system and go all the way to the Supreme Court. Clifford Durr offered to assist him. The suit was filed on behalf of five women who had been mistreated on the buses. Of the five, only two of us had been arrested: Claudette Colvin and I. The three who had not been arrested included Claudette Colvin's mother.

Meanwhile, the boycott was costing the bus company money. Every day bus after bus would go by with only one or two white riders. Then they stopped running the buses altogether. The boycott was also hurting downtown businesses, and so a group of white businessmen calling themselves Men of Montgomery decided to try to negotiate with the MIA themselves. But nothing came of those meetings.

Around the middle of February a group of white attorneys came up with an old law that prohibited boycotts, and on February 21 a grand jury handed down eighty-nine indictments against Dr. King, more than twenty other ministers, leaders of the MIA, and other citizens. I was reindicted.

We were all fingerprinted. News photographers had heard about the indictments and were there to photograph us being fingerprinted. The picture of me being fingerprinted was carried on the front page of *The New York Times.* In later years people would use that picture thinking it was from my first arrest. The MIA paid everybody's bail, and we were released and went home until the trials started. My husband was going to be a witness, and so was the woman who lived across the alley from us. Her

Rosa was just one of eighty-nine people arrested in February 1956 for boycotting without "a just cause or legal excuse." (AP/Wide World Photo)

husband was shot to death in August 1950, on the day after he came home from military service.

His name was Hilliard Brooks, and he took the bus downtown. He was accused of being drunk and disorderly, and the police shot him dead. I don't know if he had his uniform on or not. I do know that white people didn't want black veterans to wear their uniforms.

The trials began in March, and Dr. King was the first to be tried. It was March 19 and I went down to the courthouse. People crowded around and tried to get inside, but they weren't letting in anyone unless they had a seat. They wouldn't let anyone sit on the floor or stand in the aisle. There were a lot of witnesses in his defense, testifying about conditions on the buses. Our neighbor, the woman whose husband was shot, was asked if she rode the buses, and she said No. They wanted to know why she stopped riding, and she said she never rode the buses anymore after her husband was shot to death by a policeman on the bus. All of them had personal reasons. One woman got up there and talked real long. She got insulted because they wouldn't let her keep talking. She said, "I could tell you some more." People were not reluctant to speak out.

They found Dr. King guilty. He was sentenced to pay a $500 fine or serve a year at hard labor. He never did either, because the conviction was appealed successfully. He was the only one they actually tried. But of course he was more determined than ever to continue the boycott, because of the way the city of Montgomery had treated us. The people were willing. All through the spring we walked and carpooled.

There was a lot of interest in the boycott from

E. D. Nixon escorted Rosa up the courthouse steps in March 1956 for the boycott trial. (AP/Wide World Photo)

outside Montgomery now, because of all the attention from the press. I was invited to tell about what had happened to me at various churches, schools, and organizations. I did whatever I could—accepting expense money but no speaking fees—and this helped raise money for station wagons and other expenses. I spent most of the spring making appearances and speeches. Parks was concerned for my safety, but I had no unpleasant experiences.

I went to New York for the first time, at the invitation of Myles Horton, the man who had founded the Highlander Folk School in Monteagle, Tennessee. His wife had recently died, and he asked me to appear with him at some meetings in the city. I stayed with a couple named Charlotte and Stewart Meacham, who were Quakers. They showed me around the city, and I enjoyed seeing it all. After their son came back from vacation, I got a room at the Henry Street Settlement on the Lower East Side. We went to various meetings pertaining to our protest movement. People often wanted me to speak. I represented the Montgomery NAACP and met the national officers a few times.

One of those times was at the NAACP national convention in San Francisco. I remember I left New York and went out there. I had been away from home for quite a long while and I had not been able to sleep, so my nerves were pretty much fractured. But I had this interview with a reporter from a San Francisco newspaper. I was trying my best to answer this man's questions, but evidently I wasn't saying what he wanted me to say or something. He was a white reporter, and I remember one of the first things he said was, "Don't stare at me." I thought I was just looking straight at him. Well, that got me nervous. Then he announced arrogantly that he was going "to take me apart and see what made me tick." He was trying to intimidate me, and he succeeded.

I was given a cup and saucer, so the photographer the man had with him could take a picture of me as if I were sipping tea, and I remember the cup was rattling, I was shaking so. The man was being obnoxious, and I was being as polite and nice as I possibly could. Suddenly I just couldn't stand him any longer. I went into hysterics. I started screaming, and I was crying.

The reporter just walked away and went on about his business. And nobody paid me any attention. I just sat there crying. And I never will forget how Roy Wilkins, head of the NAACP, came over and sat on the couch by me and didn't say a word. But he put his arm around my shoulders and started patting me on the shoulders, and he quieted me down.

I don't know what made me go off like that. Someone told me that Autherine Lucy had her troubles keeping her composure when she was trying to integrate the University of Alabama. Somebody said that she broke down. I don't know whether she did it all the time. But that's one time I did.

I was not accustomed to so much attention. There was a time when it bothered me that I was always identified with that one incident. Then I realized that *this incident* was what brought the masses of people together to stay off the buses in Montgomery.

In June a special three-judge federal District Court ruled two to one in favor of our suit against segregation on the buses. But the city commissioners appealed the decision to the U.S. Supreme Court. We knew it would take several months for the Supreme Court to decide.

Summer came and I was back in Montgomery. We still stayed off the buses. The white people tried to break the boycott by not giving the church cars any insurance. All the churches operated the station wagons, and had their names on the sides. Without insurance, the cars could not operate legally. Every time they got insurance from a new company, the policy would suddenly be canceled. But Dr. King got in touch with a black insurance agent in Atlanta named T. M. Alexander, and T. M. Alexander got Lloyd's of London, the big insurance company in England, to write a policy for the church-operated cars.

Next, Mayor Gayle went to court to try to get an order preventing black people from gathering on street corners while waiting for the church cars. Mayor Gayle said they were a "public nuisance" because they sang loudly and bothered other people. He got a court to issue such an order, but that order came on the very same day that the U.S. Supreme Court ruled in our favor, that segregation on the Montgomery buses was unconstitutional.

That was on November 13, 1956. Dr. King called a mass meeting to tell us the news, and everybody was overjoyed. But the MIA did not tell the people to go back on the buses. The written order from the Supreme Court would not arrive for another month or so. We stayed off the buses until it was official.

In the meantime I was invited to spend a few days at the Highlander Folk School in December. That was the time when six black students in Clinton, Tennessee, were trying to integrate the schools, and they were under great pressure and danger in the white schools and without any protection. I guess they were just about to give up, and the people at Highlander invited them to Monteagle and invited me to go and see if I could encourage them not to give up and continue to hold on. Mr. Nixon accompanied me that time, and I talked to the students. There was one very small boy, I can't recall his name, who said that several white boys had jumped on him and pinned him down, and he took out his knife and cut one on the wrist, and that broke it up. But he stayed in school. After spending time at the Highlander school, they agreed to go back after New Year's.

This time when I went to Highlander, I took my

mother with me. She enjoyed the visit. But when the folks at Highlander tried to get me to move and live and work there just like Septima Poinsette Clark, Mama said No. She didn't want "to be nowhere I don't see nothing but white folks." So that ended that. Anyway, I was in no position to take off from Montgomery and stay somewhere else at that time.

I did return to Highlander for visits though. I traveled there once with the Reverend Robert Graetz,

Rosa at the Highlander School with her mother, Leona McCauley (at right), and Septima Clark (center). (Courtesy of Rosa Parks)

a white Lutheran minister in Montgomery who had supported the boycott. I remember that we had to leave Highlander when he received a call that his home had been bombed. In January 1957 his home was bombed again. The home of the Reverend Ralph Abernathy, now Dr. King's assistant, had also been bombed, along with three churches—First Baptist, Bell Street Baptist, and Hutchinson Street Baptist.

That same year I attended the twenty-fifth anniversary of Highlander Folk School with Dr. King.

Back in Montgomery, the written order from the U.S. Supreme Court arrived on December 20, and the following day we returned to the buses. The boycott had lasted more than a year. Dr. King, the Reverend Abernathy, Mr. Nixon, and Glen Smiley, one of the few white people in Montgomery who had supported the boycott, made a great show of riding the first integrated bus in Montgomery. Some of the books say I was with them, but I was not. I had planned to stay home and not ride the bus, because my mother wasn't feeling well. Somebody must have told three reporters from *Look* magazine where I lived, because they came out to the house and waited until I had finished doing whatever I was doing for my mother—fixing her breakfast or something. Then I got dressed and got into the car with them, and they drove downtown and had me get on and off buses so they could take pictures.

Rosa poses in the front seat of a Montgomery bus on December 21, 1956—the day the buses were integrated. (UPI/Bettman)

James Blake, the driver who'd had me arrested, was the driver of one of the buses I got on. He didn't want to take any honors, and I wasn't too happy about being there myself. I really could have done without that. I got on two different buses, I guess, and each time they took pictures until they were satisfied. The reporter sat behind me each time while the photographer took pictures.

James Blake never has come forward with his own feelings about what happened. Sometimes, such as on anniversaries of the bus boycott, reporters have tried to interview him, but to my knowledge they have never succeeded. I remember reading in the 1970s that some reporter tried to interview him, but his wife said he was sick and didn't want to talk about "that mess." I suspect that he never did change his attitude about African Americans and how we should be treated. Many people do not want to change, which is why it was so important for us to at least get the laws changed so we would have some protection.

Integrating the Montgomery buses did not go smoothly. Snipers fired at buses, and the city imposed curfews on the buses, not letting them run after five P.M., which meant that people who worked from nine to five couldn't ride the buses home. A group of whites tried to form a whites-only bus line, but that didn't work. The homes and churches of some ministers were bombed, as I mentioned. But eventually most of the violence died down. Black people were not going to be scared off the buses any more than they were going to be scared onto them when they refused to ride.

African Americans in other cities, like Birmingham, Alabama, and Tallahassee, Florida, started their own boycotts of the segregated buses. The direct-action civil-rights movement had begun.

11

We Move to Detroit

I didn't stay in Montgomery long after the bus boycott ended. My brother made arrangements for us
to move, because he was very concerned for our
safety in Alabama. We did suffer some harassment.

The threatening telephone calls continued even
after the Supreme Court decision. My husband slept
with a gun nearby for a time. Bertha Butler, a close
friend of ours in Montgomery, says that my mother
would call her some nights and talk for long periods
just to jam the lines so the hate calls couldn't get
through for a while. Once, when I was on the street,
a white man recognized me and made a hateful re-
mark. My picture had been in the papers, and it was
doubtful that I could ever get a regular job in a white
business in Montgomery.

My brother had moved to Detroit after World War
II. He never went back to Alabama after he left, never
visited at all. He told us he would see that we got
settled up there, and so we did move to Detroit in
1957. By that time the calls and the harassment had

pretty much subsided, but we thought life would be better for us in Detroit.

The day before we left, our friends in Montgomery held an event for us and collected some money as a going-away present. It was about eight hundred dollars, and we were grateful to have it, because we didn't have much money. My brother, Sylvester, had rented an upper apartment for us on Euclid Avenue in Detroit, and my husband and my mother and I moved in there.

I was still traveling around, making appearances. About a month after we moved to Detroit, I went to Boston, Massachusetts. There I met the president of Hampton Institute, a black college in Hampton, Virginia. He asked me if I would accept a job as a hostess at Holly Tree Inn, which was the residence and guest house on the campus. I would be in charge of the off-the-campus guests and also the men and women, faculty and staff, who lived there. Four women worked half days cleaning the rooms, and I would be in charge of them. I accepted the position at Hampton hoping that there would be a place for my husband and mother as well, but it didn't work out. They remained in Detroit. Neither was well, although Parks did pretty good and went to school to get his barber's license while I was gone. The state of Michigan required barbers to be licensed. He got a job as a combination instructor and maintenance man at a barber college. He also registered to vote for the first time in his life. I was lonely and disliked being separated from my family.

I was at Hampton Institute when Martin Luther King, Jr., was stabbed in New York City in the summer of 1958. I remember I was reading *Stride Toward Freedom*, his first book, which he had personally autographed for me, when I heard the news. He had been signing copies of that book in a bookstore in New York when a deranged woman stepped up to him and stabbed him. He was in very serious condition in the hospital.

That was a terrible shock to me. I became hysterical and I cried. I was very relieved when the operation was successful and he was all right.

It was difficult going through that experience alone. I was not that well myself while I was at Hampton. During the Christmas holiday when I went back to Detroit, I went to a doctor for minor surgery. I did inquire around Hampton to see if I could get housing for all of us and get my husband a job at the local barbershop for blacks, but I wasn't successful at either one. There was an apartment in the Holly Tree Inn Annex that I asked to have, but they never did give consent for me to use it. They did not say exactly why, but I think they wanted to use it for faculty.

My husband and my mother missed me a lot, and I just felt that it was too much for me to try to remain at Hampton alone and be concerned about them. At Hampton they really wanted me to stay, and I had mixed feelings about leaving, because I liked my job and it was a beautiful campus. But I felt I should go back to Detroit.

Back in Detroit I worked in the home of a seamstress friend, and then later I got a job at a small clothing factory on the west side of the city. In 1961 we moved to a lower apartment on Virginia Park.

I was still traveling around quite a bit, speaking about the bus boycott and the civil-rights movement, which had really gotten active by this time. Dr. King and other ministers had formed the Southern Christian Leadership Conference (SCLC) to fight against segregation in other areas of southern life. I went back south to attend SCLC conventions, and when there was a big march or demonstration, I was there.

I remember one SCLC convention in particular. It was held in Birmingham, Alabama, one of the most viciously segregated cities. That's where whites bombed a church and killed four little black girls. I was sitting in the audience, near the stage. Dr. King was closing the convention with some announcements when a white man from the audience jumped up on the stage and hit Dr. King in the face with his fist, spinning him halfway around. It took everybody by surprise, and before anyone could react, the man was hitting Dr. King again. Dr. King was trying to shield himself from the blows. And then suddenly Dr. King turned around to face the man and just dropped his hands by his sides. The white man was so surprised that he just stared for a moment, long enough for the Reverend Wyatt Tee Walker and some others to get between them.

Dr. King yelled, "Don't touch him! We have to pray for him." Then he started talking quietly to the man, and he kept talking as the man was slowly led off the stage. There seemed to be more attention devoted to calming the man down than to looking after Dr. King.

I went backstage and offered him two aspirins and a Coca-Cola, my remedy for a headache. He was holding a handkerchief full of ice against his face. He later told the convention that he and the man had talked and that the man was a member of the American Nazi Party. The American Nazi Party is a very racist organization. But Dr. King refused to press charges against that man. That, for many of us, was proof that Dr. King believed so completely in nonviolence that it was even stronger than his instinct to protect himself from attack.

I was also at the 1963 March on Washington to push for federal civil-rights laws. Women were not allowed to play much of a role. The March planning committee didn't want Coretta Scott King and the other wives of the male leaders to march with their husbands. Instead there was a separate procession for them. There were also no female speakers on the program, the one where Dr. King gave his famous "I Have a Dream" speech in front of the Lincoln Memorial.

But there was a "Tribute to Women" in which A. Philip Randolph, one of the organizers of the March and the founder of the Brotherhood of Sleeping Car Porters, introduced some of the women who had participated in the struggle, and I was one of them. Another was Josephine Baker, the beautiful dancer and singer who had spent most of her life in Europe but who had stood up for equal rights when she was in the United States. She flew over from Paris just for the March. Marian Anderson sang "He's Got the Whole World in His Hands," and Mahalia Jackson sang "I Been 'Buked and I Been Scorned." Those of us who did not sing didn't get to say anything, as I recall—except for Lena Horne, who was introduced and who then stood and loudly proclaimed, "Freedom." Nowadays, women wouldn't stand for being kept so much in the background, but back then women's rights hadn't become a popular cause yet.

I spoke at the SCLC's seventh annual convention in Richmond, Virginia, the following month. Other people gave reports about the civil-rights movement in a variety of cities. By this time black people in cities and towns all over the South were organizing and demonstrating against segregation.

The civil-rights movement was having a big effect. It didn't change the hearts and minds of many white southerners, but it did make a difference to the politicians in Washington, D.C. The president at that time was Lyndon Baines Johnson, born and raised in Texas. It was he who pushed through the 1964 Civil Rights Act, the most far-reaching legislation since the Reconstruction period after the Civil War. It aimed to guarantee blacks the right to vote and to use public accommodations, and provided for the federal government to prosecute those who did not obey this law. When he signed that act into law, President Johnson said, "We shall overcome," using the words of a song that we had sung many times during the Montgomery bus boycott and that black and white civil-rights workers had sung many times throughout the later struggle.

That Civil Rights Act of 1964 did not solve all our problems. But it gave black people some protection, and some way to get redress for unfair treatment. There were still more rights to win, and the civil-rights movement continued.

In the beginning of 1965 Dr. King and the SCLC decided to stage a campaign of demonstrations in Selma, Alabama, where they weren't having much progress in getting black people registered to vote. They decided to pack the jails by deliberately getting themselves arrested, and that got the local police angry. In early February Selma's Sheriff Jim Clark and his men surrounded a group of about 150 children who were demonstrating downtown. They herded them out of town like cattle, making them trot along the country roads and using electric cattle prods to force them to keep up the pace. The TV news carried the scene, and that got civil-rights activists angry. It also broadened the support of the civil-rights movement among whites across the nation. People started going to Selma from all parts of the country. Dr. King decided to call for a mass march from Selma to Montgomery, about fifty miles away. It was set for March 7, 1965.

The SCLC applied for a march permit, and got approval to have a maximum of three hundred marchers on the two-lane segments of Highway 80 between the two cities. On the four-lane sections, closer to Selma and to Montgomery, there could be an unlimited number of marchers. I was invited to join the march for the last lap into downtown Montgomery.

The marchers started out from Brown's Chapel in Selma on a Sunday, and it took them until Wednesday night to cover the fifty miles to the outskirts of Montgomery. The march was highly organized. There would be up to three thousand people in the places where Highway 80 was four lanes, but no more than three hundred when it was just two lanes across. The march organizers had set up campsites and plenty of food and clothing. People like Dick Gregory, the comedian who was famous for going

The Selma-to-Montgomery march. From left to right: Rosa; the Reverend Ralph David Abernathy; Mrs. Juanita Abernathy; Ambassador Ralph Bunche; Dr. Martin Luther King, Jr.; Mrs. Jean Young; Mrs. Coretta Scott King; and the Reverend L. V. Reese. (Photo by Elaine Tomlin/Courtesy of SCLA)

on hunger strikes to call attention to civil-rights issues and the plight of the poor, and Harry Belafonte, the singer, entertained the marchers where they camped at night. They even had people wearing different-colored jackets to signify if they had marched all the way from Selma.

Thursday was the day for the final march to the capitol building, and that's when I joined the march. There were a lot of important people on that lap, but Mr. E. D. Nixon was not one of them. He didn't go for the march at all, didn't think that much of it. He was standing on the side. I may have stood with him for a while, one of the times they put me out.

Being on that march was a strange experience. It seemed like such a short time that I had been out of Alabama, but so many young people had grown up in that time. They didn't know who I was and couldn't care less about me because they didn't know me. Marchers on that final lap were supposed to be wearing special-colored jackets or other clothing, and I wasn't wearing the right color. They just kept putting me out of the march, telling me I wasn't supposed to be in it. I got put out of that march three or four different times. Whenever they would put me out, I would just stand on the sidelines until somebody would pass by and say, "Mrs. Parks, come on and get in the march." I would say, "I *was* in it, but they put me out."

Then they'd say, "Well, come on and march with me this time."

I remember I marched for a while with Dick Gregory's wife, Lillian. I marched with the gospel singer Odetta. But somehow or another I couldn't hold on to them, or couldn't keep up with them, and then some of those youngsters just sort of pushed me out of the way. But I kept getting back in anyway and I struggled through that crowd until I walked those eight miles to the capitol.

When we got downtown, someone did have me go up to the front of the line, and I had my picture taken with Roy Wilkins, head of the NAACP, and Ralph Bunche, the first black American winner of the Nobel Peace Prize, and other important people. Mostly I remember being put out of that march.

The other thing I remember about that day is that when we got to the capitol building, there were so many hostile white people jeering and shouting at us. We might have integrated the buses, but there was a lot more to be done in Montgomery to bring about peace between the races.

And then we heard the news about Mrs. Viola Liuzzo being murdered. She was from Detroit, although I didn't know her. She was a white housewife who felt strongly about civil rights and who took it upon herself to drive down to Alabama and see if she could help out on the Selma-to-Montgomery march. She and a young black volunteer were driving through Lowndes County on their way to Montgomery to help carry the marchers back to Selma when a carload of Ku Klux Klansmen pulled up next to her and shot her.

The night before I heard the news, I had a strange dream. I hadn't been able to sleep very much. I grew up being an insomniac at times, and that was one of the nights I had trouble getting to sleep. When I did fall asleep, I had this very, very strange dream. My husband and I were out in a field someplace, and there was a large billboard standing there. I saw somebody with a gun, and I was trying to tell my husband, "Parks, hurry up and get out of the way, they might shoot you." A man dressed in blue-jean overalls—I didn't know him—stepped from behind this billboard. I was at one end and he was at the other, and he pointed the gun to fire directly at me, and I woke up. When I woke up, I turned on the TV, and that's when I learned that Mrs. Liuzzo had been shot.

I guess it was a kind of premonition, because I remember feeling that something was not right. Even though the march was over, I felt that everything was not well. She was from Detroit, and for some reason nobody had warned her that she should not be going back and forth with black people in her car at night. It was very shocking, but in the South at that time, it was just one of those things in life you might as well expect.

President Lyndon B. Johnson (right) with (from left): Congressman Walter Fauntroy, Dr. Martin Luther King, Jr., and the Reverend Ralph David Abernathy, after signing the Voting Rights Act in 1965. (Photo by Y. R. Okamoto/Courtesy of LBJ Library)

I attended a memorial service for Viola Liuzzo, where I met her husband and children.

In August of that year, 1965, President Johnson signed into law the Voting Rights Act. It provided that blacks who were denied the chance to register to vote by local officials could get registered by federal examiners. This was one more law to help the black people of the South, and it was an important one.

Both these laws were a direct result of nonviolent protests on the part of black people and their white supporters. Dr. King believed very strongly in the concept of nonviolence. He had read a great deal about the way Mohandas Gandhi in India had used nonviolent demonstrations to gain the independence of the Indian people from Great Britain. Gandhi had said not to fight back, and Dr. King said not to fight back, and I believe that is the only way African Americans were able to win so many victories over segregation.

When I think back to the times of my growing up and the problems that we had, I realize we didn't know anything about nonviolence even though we didn't get into anything that would bring about lynching. We always felt that if you talked violently and said what you would do if they did something to you, that did more good than nonviolence. I mentioned earlier what my grandmother said when I was very young, but I just couldn't accept being pushed even at the cost of my life. I was raised to be proud, and it had worked for me to stand up aggressively for myself. I know my husband said that when he was a teenager, or a very young man, in his hometown in eastern Alabama, he hadn't known anything about nonviolence either. He knew that he would have to talk up for himself if he wanted to protect himself.

Most of the black people in Montgomery had

similar feelings. On an individual level, nonviolence could be mistaken for cowardice. The concept of mass nonviolent action was something new and very controversial. Some people thought it was too risky and would invite more violence. No one had tried it before in the United States. I had read about Gandhi in India, but I had never applied his philosophy to our individual protests. However, with the entire African-American population of Montgomery going the nonviolent way, I saw that the tactic could be successful. So were the other protests in those days when the fight was against segregation.

To this day, I am not an absolute supporter of nonviolence in all situations. But I strongly believe that the civil-rights movement of the 1950s and 1960s could never have been so successful without Dr. King and his firm belief in nonviolence.

12

The Years Since

In 1964 John Conyers, an African-American attorney who had worked as a legislative assistant to Congressman John Dingle, was a candidate for Congress from the First Congressional District in Michigan. He asked for my endorsement of his candidacy, and I gave it. I liked what he had to say and the legislation he wanted to pass. After he won the election, he asked me to work for him in his office in Detroit. I started on March 1, 1965, not long before the Selma-to-Montgomery march. I worked for him until I retired on September 30, 1988. I was a receptionist and office assistant, and I helped get housing for people who were homeless and things like that.

The same year I started working for John Conyers, Malcolm X was shot. I didn't know him, even though the home base of the Black Muslims was in Detroit, where they had their Temple Number 1. By the time we moved to Detroit, he was in New York heading the big temple there. The Black Muslims preached hatred of white people, and I never went along with hatred of anybody. But the Muslims were very successful at converting men in jail and getting them to lead clean lives after they got out. They were very serious about black people doing for themselves, having their own businesses and strong family relationships.

Malcolm X was converted to the Muslims while in jail. He had been a career criminal who went by the nickname "Detroit Red." Becoming a Black Muslim changed his whole life. But Malcolm X went to Mecca in Saudi Arabia, where the original Muslim religion has its base, and he learned that Muslims in other parts of the world weren't racist and did not preach hatred of white people. He left the Black Muslims. When he was shot in February 1965, he was trying to build a new organization that did not preach hatred.

I met him the week before he died. He had come to Detroit to speak, and I was sitting in the front row. His home in New York had been firebombed and all his clothes had been damaged by water and smoke, but he came to Detroit anyway because he'd made a commitment. I spoke to him and he autographed the program for me. He had changed his manner of speaking and the way he expressed himself. I had heard him speak before, but now his message was altogether different. I had a lot of admiration for him, considering his background and where he came from and his having had to struggle so hard just to reach the point of being respected as a leader of the Black Muslims. He was a very brilliant man. Even when he was with the Black Muslims, I didn't disagree with him altogether.

I remember him talking about violence. He spoke about the expression "Father, forgive them, for they know not what they do," which is what Jesus Christ said when he was on the cross. Dr. King used to say that black people should receive brutality with love, and I believed that this was a goal to work for. But I couldn't reach that point in my mind at all, even though I know that the strategy Dr. King used probably was the better one for the masses of people in Montgomery than trying to retaliate without any weapons or ammunition.

Malcolm wasn't a supporter of nonviolence either. Referring to what Dr. King liked to say about people not knowing what they do, he used to say of the white racists who attacked nonviolent demonstrators for civil rights, "Not only did they know what they were doing, but they were *experts* at it."

Three years after I started working in John Conyers' office, Dr. King was shot and killed on April 4, 1968. I remember my mother and I were listening to the radio. It was approaching Easter time, and usually Dr. King would broadcast his sermons during the Lenten season. But this time Dr. King was in Memphis, Tennessee, where he had promised to participate in a march in support of the black garbage collectors. Somebody else came on the radio instead. It was one of the ministers who had a very great dislike for Dr. King, I think because of his popularity and how people gravitated to him. My mother and I were both listening and saying, "Well, there's Reverend King's enemy on the air." And right in the midst of this minister's speech, the program was interrupted to say that Dr. King had been shot. It was very devastating.

Shortly afterward the report came over the radio that the shooting was fatal. For some reason, that didn't affect me as much as the first attack, when he was stabbed. When he was stabbed, I was shocked at the idea that anyone would try to hurt him. By the time he was assassinated, I had come to realize that there were people who wished him harm. I was deeply grieved. Mama and I wept quietly together.

I got ready to go to Memphis. Louise Tappes, a friend in Detroit, and I were traveling together at that time, since Parks wasn't much for traveling. We got together with some other people and went to Memphis for the march that Dr. King was to have participated in. Mr. Sheldon Tappes, Louise's husband, who was a labor leader for the United Auto Workers union, made the arrangements. Harry Belafonte, the singer, took me to Atlanta for Dr.

King's funeral in a private plane. Senator Robert Kennedy and his wife, Ethel, were at the funeral. I met them before the funeral at the home of Mrs. King.

Not long afterward I had a dream about Dr. King. He was going up a chimney above a great big fireplace, sitting on kind of a round seat. He was facing me, and he had on work clothing, a blue-jeans outfit. And facing him, with his back to me, was a young white man with dark hair and a small build. I didn't think much about it. But then in June, two months later, Robert Kennedy was assassinated. And then I remembered the dream.

It just seemed like we were losing everybody we thought was good.

I remember the 1970s as a time when I was losing the people I loved best. My husband, mother, and brother were all sick, and there was a time when I was traveling every day to three different hospitals to visit them. I had to quit working full-time and work only part-time. Parks died in 1977, when he was seventy-four, after a five-year struggle against cancer. My brother, Sylvester, died three months after that, also of cancer. Mama was ill with cancer too, and after my husband died I had to put her in a nursing home for a year, because I wasn't able to give her the proper care and work too. But I visited her for breakfast, lunch, and dinner every day, seven days a week.

After I moved into an apartment building for senior citizens in 1978, I took my mother out of the nursing home and cared for her at home until she died in 1979 at the age of ninety-one.

My health wasn't too good at that time either, but I kept on working. I couldn't do everything I wanted to do, but I did what I could.

One thing that I had long wanted to do was to start some kind of organization to help young people. In 1987 I founded the Rosa and Raymond Parks

Rosa Parks at a Detroit school during Black History Week. (Courtesy of Rosa Parks)

Institute for Self-Development, and I have been working very hard to raise money for that.

I envision the institute as a community-center environment that will offer programs for youth to help them continue their education and have hope for the future. That is a goal that has always been close to my heart. It was something that my husband also talked about many times, for he had not been able to get an education as a youngster. Through the institute, I hope to give scholarships to deserving young people and to offer courses in communications skills, economic skills, political awareness, and health awareness that will help them realize their highest potential and provide the marketable skills that will enable them to be contributing, productive citizens. I would like them to have the same sense of hope, dignity, and pride that was instilled in me by my family and my teachers.

Elaine Steele is Executive Director and co-founder of the Institute. She also makes all the arrangements and travels with me when I am invited to speak or appear for many different organizations around the country. That happens quite a lot, even though it has now been more than thirty years since the Montgomery bus boycott.

It would be difficult to provide a complete list of all the cities and towns and organizations that have honored me, or invited me to be part of some special event or another. I would surely leave out some, and I would not want anyone to feel slighted. But there are two occasions that I would like to mention when I have been honored in Montgomery, Alabama, where it all started.

The bus on which I was arrested back on December 1955 was part of the Cleveland Avenue line. Today, Cleveland Avenue is named Rosa Parks Boulevard.

Raymond Parks, Louise Tappes, Rosa, Septima Clark, and Coretta Scott King gathered in Detroit, 1965, for the Women's Political Action Committee to honor Rosa.
(Courtesy of Rosa Parks)

Twelfth Street in Detroit, 1975, is renamed Rosa Parks Boulevard.
(Courtesy of Rosa Parks)

In November 1989 a memorial was dedicated in
Montgomery. Erected by the Southern Poverty Law
Center, the sculpture was designed by Maya Lin,
the architect who created the Vietnam War Memorial in Washington, D.C. The names of forty men
and women who were killed in the civil-rights
movement are etched on a circular black granite ta-

184

ble that is in front of a curving wall. Water cascades down the wall, forming a thin film over these words of Dr. King's:

> ". . . until justice rolls down like waters and righteousness like a mighty stream."

I was very proud to have been invited to the dedication of that very special memorial.

As time has gone by, people have made my place in the history of the civil-rights movement bigger and bigger. They call me the Mother of the Civil Rights Movement and the Patron Saint of the Civil Rights Movement. I have more honorary degrees and plaques and awards than I can count, and I appreciate and cherish every single one of them. Interviewers still only want to talk about that one evening in 1955 when I refused to give up my seat on the bus. Organizations still want to give me awards for that one act more than thirty years ago. I am happy to go wherever I am invited and to accept whatever honors are given me. I understand that I am a symbol.

But I have never gotten used to being a "public person." I don't especially care for my health to be too much of a public thing. When you get older, it is just natural to decline somewhat. Nowadays when I go into the hospital, the papers report it. They reported it when I had a pacemaker put in at Johns Hopkins Hospital in Baltimore in 1988, and when I suffered chest palpitations in February 1989 and had to be hospitalized again. It is nice, though, when people all across the country send me cards and flowers and get-well wishes.

My life has changed a great deal since 1955. I've done a lot more traveling than I know I would have done, and I have met a lot of people I would not have otherwise met. Some people have me believe, when they talk with me, that I have influenced their lives in many ways.

I look back now and realize that since that evening on the bus in Montgomery, Alabama, we have made a lot of progress in some ways. Young people can go to register to vote without being threatened and can vote without feeling apprehensive. There are no signs on public water fountains saying "Colored" and "White." There are big cities with black mayors, and small towns with black mayors and chiefs of police. Tom Bradley was elected the first African-American mayor of a major American city. Douglas L. Wilder was elected governor of Virginia, the first black governor of a state ever elected. And thirty years ago no one would have believed that Jesse Jackson, a black man, could run for president of the United States and get white votes in the state primary elections.

All those laws against segregation have been passed, and all that progress has been made. But a whole lot of white people's hearts have not been changed. Dr. King used to talk about the fact that if a law was changed, it might not change hearts but it would offer some protection. He was right. We now have some protection, but there is still much racism and racial violence.

In recent years there has been a resurgence of reactionary attitudes. I am troubled by the recent decisions of the Supreme Court that make it harder to prove a pattern of racial discrimination in employment and by the fact that the national government does not seem very interested in pursuing violations of civil rights. What troubles me is that so many young people, including college students, have come out for white supremacy and that there have been more and more incidents of racism and racial violence on college campuses. It has not been widespread, but still it is troublesome. It seems like we still have a long way to go.

Sometimes I do feel pretty sad about some of the events that have taken place recently. I try to keep hope alive anyway, but that's not always the easiest thing to do. I have spent over half my life teaching love and brotherhood, and I feel that it is better to continue to try to teach or live equality and love than it would be to have hatred or prejudice. Everyone living together in peace and harmony and love

... that's the goal that we seek, and I think that the more people there are who reach that state of mind, the better we will all be.

Portrait of Rosa Parks, 1980s. (Courtesy of Rosa Parks)

CHRONOLOGY

February 4, 1913	Rosa McCauley born in Tuskegee, Alabama
1918	Enters school in Pine Level, Alabama
1924	Begins attending school in Montgomery
1929	Leaves school to care for grandmother
December 1932	Marries Raymond Parks in Pine Level, Alabama
1933	Receives high school degree
December 1943	Becomes secretary of NAACP
1943	Tries to register to vote and is denied
	Put off bus for the first time for not entering at the back
1944	Tries a second time to register to vote and is denied again
1945	Finally receives certificate for voting
1949	Adviser to the NAACP Youth Council
Summer 1955	Attends workshop at Highlander Folk School in Monteagle, Tennessee, for the first time
August 1955	Meets Dr. Martin Luther King, Jr.
December 1, 1955	Arrested for not giving up her seat to a white man on a bus in Montgomery
December 5, 1955	Stands trial; found guilty
	Attends meeting of ministers who have formed the Montgomery Improvement Association
	Start of Montgomery, Alabama, Bus Boycott
January 1956	Loses job at Montgomery Fair department store
February 21, 1956	Reindicted for boycotting
November 13, 1956	Segregation on buses in Montgomery declared unconstitutional by United States Supreme Court
December 21, 1956	Boycotters return to buses
1957	Rosa Parks moves to Detroit
1963	Attends Civil Rights March on Washington
	Speaks at SCLC's annual convention
March 1965	Participates in Selma-to-Montgomery march
1965	Begins working for Congressman John Conyers in Detroit
1977	Raymond Parks dies
1979	Leona McCauley, Rosa's mother, dies
1987	Founds the Rosa and Raymond Parks Institute for Self-Development
September 1988	Retires from working for John Conyers
November 1989	Attends dedication of Civil Rights memorial in Montgomery, Alabama
February 28, 1991	Bust of Rosa Parks unveiled at Smithsonian

INDEX

Italicized page numbers refer to photographs

Index